House Calls 101

The Only Book You'll Ever Need to
Start Your Housecall Practice

Dr. Scharmaine Lawson, NP

Published by A DrNurse Publishing House New Orleans, Louisiana

A DrNURSE
PUBLISHING HOUSE

Published by

A DrNurse Publishing House

7041 Canal Blvd., New Orleans, La. 70124

www.DrLawsonNP.com

ISBN: 978-1-945088-39-1

Library of Congress Control Number: 2015933564

This book is printed on acid-free paper.

Printed in the United States of America

Dedication

Dear Skylar Rose, and Wyatt Shane, your ability to love me in spite of my many moods while writing continues to keep me suspended in awe and total adoration of you.

Dear Grandma, I miss you more than life. Thank you for the memories and your abiding spirit, which lives in me. You would be proud of the woman I've become because of your love, rearing, and nurturing. You adopted me at four-months old when you were at the tender age of 60 and somehow always "knew" that I would make something out of myself. I'm so glad you believed in me.

Contents

꧁

Preface

I see my patients in my New Orleans practice where they live—no matter where that may be. I am always saying, "It doesn't matter where they are; if they need me, I need to be there with them."

I am guilty of having a missionary zeal for my patients' well-being. As the CEO of Advanced Clinical Consultants (ACC), a network of home-visiting health-care providers who take the clinic to their patients, I put in a full day and then some, seeing and consulting with patients all over the New Orleans area, all while administering my growing business on the fly.

My path to a home healthcare nurse practitioner (NP) practice started while I was pursuing my NP degree at Tennessee State University, where I joined humanitarian mission trips to the Dominican Republic and Puerto Rico.

These experiences whetted my appetite for meeting very human needs related to primary care in the community— and for my own community, back home in New Orleans.

I decided to take my boards in New Orleans and settle down into a practice in 2002. I developed a passion for geriatric care and eventually landed a consultancy position, working with various doctors and filling in as needed with their practices.

The germ of the idea that led to ACC came in late 2004. A home care agency approached me about doing home health care as an NP. It just made sense. I soon began networking with other home care providers I knew. I also began creating my own forms, based on ideas that my colleagues shared with me. Piece by piece, I stepped into my own practice, forming ACC as a limited-liability corporation in March 2005.

At about that time, I also started making use of my pocket personal digital assistant (PDA) to store my patient files. It made life much simpler. From March to August 2005, my practice grew from 15 to 100 patients. I even set up shop in a cottage behind my home.

Then came August 27, 2005: Hurricane Katrina. Like many city natives, my fiancé, his mother, and I boarded up the house and made plans to stay in a hotel in the north of the city. As it became apparent that Katrina was going to be an epic disaster, we realized it was acutely necessary for us to leave the city.

After evacuating to Texas, one thing that kept me

from going too crazy with boredom while I was in exile in San Antonio was that I was needed—and my anal-retentive habit of keeping my records in my PDA saved the day for many of my precious patients. I got calls from healthcare providers all over the country who were seeing my displaced patients. I was able to answer their questions and to share the information they needed to provide treatment. It was how I stayed involved in my patients' care and lives, even though I was hundreds of miles away from them.

Two short months after that huge natural disaster, in October 2005, I returned home to New Orleans, finding that our home was still floating in five feet of water, and we could get there only by boat. It was a gut-wrenching thing to see, simply devastating, but at least I was back home and could start seeing clients.

There were many who needed primary care ASAP. I did a lot of traveling at that time. Many, many older folks needed home care—and much more—at this time, because so many were and are homebound, or even bedbound. I had to get to them, no matter what. There was always a sense of urgency about my stride through the neighborhoods during this time because everything was so unpredictable. For instance, it would not be uncommon to make a visit to see one elderly person and to soon start to get requests from several family members who were camped out in the home waiting to know the conditions of their own homes. Entire families were displaced and left confused about where to find healthcare and where to fill prescriptions. This was where my skills as an NP came into play. My skill sets were in high demand. I threw myself into visiting 40–50 patients a day.

This somehow allowed me to forget about the pain of losing so many of my own personal belongings. Helping others allows you to forget about self. These selfless actions made me focus on helping as many as possible, however I could make that happen. It was also not uncommon for me to hear gunfire while making a house call, but I would just duck, walk really fast, and slip into the next patient's home.

Looking back on all this, I think I was pretty courageous or downright crazy, but I survived to tell the story. That's all that matters. The point is, you should be willing to provide health care anywhere when you have the skill set. That's my opinion, and I'm sticking to it. Ten years later, I still feel a sense of urgency when it comes to getting an elderly person the health care he or she deserves and needs. I'm glad the fire is still there. I hope it never leaves. This fire makes it easy to go to work. It's called passion.

Before Katrina hit, I had been one of maybe one or two doctors and two NPs making house calls in New Orleans and was the first NP to establish a house-call practice in the state of Louisiana. In the storm's wake, I was it. I got busy really fast delivering healthcare to hundreds.

I also started building a network with other home providers—a pharmacist who delivered medicines, plus a podiatrist and an optometrist who also made house calls—and we shared patients. They were as committed as I was to going where we were needed. This meant travel into dangerous areas where there was no electricity or running water, and sometimes gaping holes in the floors of homes. After the waters and winds of Katrina subsided, the damage certainly didn't. I saw patients in badly damaged homes, FEMA trailers, or anywhere else they needed me. I've treated patients on rooftops, on porches, in attics, even in homes that were stripped to the stud posts, and I would do it all over again if it were needed.

Today, ACC treats several thousand patients, all elderly and disabled—and many making only about

$300–$400 a month. They are below the poverty line. We probably see one thousand of those actively. And that's not all I have on my plate, either. I recently founded a publishing company to launch my many literary projects. I've been named a 2013 *New Orleans City Business* magazine Healthcare Hero, and I was inducted in 2012 into the prestigious Fellows of the American Association of Nurse Practitioners. In the meantime, I continue to make myself at home as the primary source of health care for the people who need me most.

I have wanted to write this book series for a very long time now. It is the first of several planned House Call 101 book installments. Each book is planned to build on the previous book and to include updated billing codes and other pertinent information for house- call practitioners. My favorite parts of this series are the patient stories, because these are about actual patients who have consented to have their stories told. Whether you are new to house calls, a veteran house-call provider, or just reading out of curiosity, this book includes something for you. Whatever your reason for purchasing this book, I certainly hope it becomes your go-to reference about house calls.

Introduction

❖

I didn't wake up one day with the overwhelming desire to be a business owner or to provide house calls. This was not my intention, but somewhere along the way between Hurricane Katrina, realizing that house calls were indeed a niche market, and raising my young family, I fell in love with the idea of providing primary care in people's homes. It is now my passion. When you're passionate about something, you want to tell everybody about it and get as many folks excited about it as you possibly can. This is why I'm writing this book.

My Story: I was interested in home visits for personal reasons. My grandmother raised me, and after she became frail in 1996, I really needed someone to visit her in our home to provide primary care. She was 89-years-old, and I was desperate for help. This was not readily available at the time, however. It would have made a world of difference to us. I would have been able to continue to work, and she possibly could have skipped admission to a nursing home. I was just like most people trying to find a way to care for an aging parent without utilizing the option of a nursing home. In the end, we were not able to avoid using a nursing home, and I remain firm in believing that if we would have had that layer of a house-call provider, she may have been able to remain in the home which could have ultimately extended her life and time with me.

When I first started to research the Internet for information about how to start a house-call practice, I got, at best, two possible hits on the subject. There was just nothing available for NPs looking to get into this business, because very few were providing house calls. To date, I can find a little more than two hits on the subject matter, but still not much. As excited as I am about this interest of mine, my "baby," I have to add my perspective to the house-call annals. My goal with this book is to inform the reader about what it's like to make a house call, to arm the reader with practical knowledge necessary for business sustainability, and to encourage the reader to create a passion for house calls that is as great as mine.

I love house calls, and the privilege of serving people in their homes, so much that I often follow or continue to care for people until they die. That's right. I will continue to care for and visit a person through home health and then on to hospice, all in the comfort of their homes when possible. Isn't this what nursing and medicine is all about? We are charged to care for the vulnerable, the weak, and the homeless, and to do no harm until we've done all we can do.

I am a board-certified family nurse practitioner (FNP), and I have written this book from my perspective as an NP celebrating 10 years of a successful house-call practice in New Orleans, Louisiana; hence, I have written it primarily for NPs, but many of the chapters are applicable to other healthcare providers, such as physician assistants (PAs) and physicians (MDs) as well, because NPs/PAs and MDs use the same CPT and ICD9 coding for billing and reimbursement. This book delves deep into the house-call billing and coding necessary for establishing and, more importantly, maintaining a viable house-call practice; however, it is not to be mistaken for a medical billing book. Many areas regarding the field of home medicine will be discussed. If you are a registered nurse (RN) or licensed practical nurse (LPN), there are some areas that may be of special interest to you, such as the safety chapter, or the personal stories I have included, but the billing, coding, and reimbursement sections are solely for those providers who are able to assess, diagnose, prescribe, and treat comorbidities commonly seen in various home- bound patients.

The History of the House Call

Several years ago, most doctor/provider visits were made in patients' homes. As technology evolved, however, hospitals began to offer better diagnostic and treatment tools. X-ray equipment and laboratory testing changed the way medicine was practiced. Healthcare providers started bringing patients to the hospital to take advantage of these diagnostic tools. Ultimately, providers set up offices with this high-tech equipment and patients flocked to see them, and then things got really efficient. Doctors could "pack" people in their rooms and see 20 to 30 patients a day! Making house calls was less efficient, but some practitioners still tried to meet their patients' needs by providing house calls when their patients were very sick or bedbound. Now, many more hospitals are turning to house calls in an effort to reduce frequent hospitalizations and readmission rates (Emanuel, 2013).

Medical costs began to soar as more and more expensive tests, treatments, and medicines became available. In an effort to cut costs, Medicare and managed care started to reimburse less for a provider's time and instead paid mostly by the procedure performed. As our nation's medical costs continued to increase, primary care providers' reimbursement continued to decrease. Now, providers are strained to work longer days and see more patients just to cover the costs of running their practices. In most cases, many providers simply cannot afford to make home visits.

The sickest patients are really not receiving the care they need. If their conditions worsen and they cannot be seen soon enough, they are eventually hospitalized. The severity of their illnesses often leaves them weakened and thus requiring pro- longed rehabilitation in facilities. Many of these fragile patients fail to make complete recoveries, and they bounce around among hospitals, skilled-nursing facilities, rehab facilities, and, eventually, home. Emergency rooms and urgent-care clinics are crowded with exorbitant emergency medical conditions that prompt house calls could have prevented—or, at the very least, lessened the severity of. With increasing frequency, emergency rooms are providing non-emergent care for patients who have no other access to care (Shulman, 2007).

In the late 1990s, Medicare increased the reimbursement for house calls. This allowed the start of house call-based practices, because what a medical practitioner loses in efficiency of having to go from patient home to patient home, he or she saves in overhead costs of running a clinic. The real change related to the increase in house-call usage came with portable technology. Now a provider can bring clinical tools (X-rays, laboratory tests, EKGs, and other portable diagnostics) to the patient's home. In addition, with electronic health records (EHRs), a healthcare provider can carry every patient's medical file, making it easier to attend urgent calls (Shulman, 2007).

House Calls Today, and Where NPs Stand in Home Health

House calls are back and bring many benefits, including that Medicare saves money from hospitalizations and emergency room visits, physicians can choose whether they want to make 10 house calls or see 30 patients in an office each day, and, most importantly, quality care can go to the very patients who need it most. Currently, providers who accept Medicare Part B are required to manage and directly provide progressively more sophisticated home visits.

More than 80% of Americans older than 50 years wish to remain in their homes indefinitely, rather than moving to assisted-living or nursing-care facilities, even in the event of disabling illness. More than 75% of adults 55 years and older moved into their current residences before 2000. Older buildings seldom include features that assist persons with disabilities in performing activities of daily living (ADLs). Research shows that environmental and technological interventions in the homes of frail older persons slow functional decline compared with home care without these interventions, and that these interventions reduce personal- care expenditures that would be used for institutional care (e.g., nursing, case worker visits; Unwin, Andrews, Andrews, & Hanson, 2009).

Home health agencies and hospice care entities are still unable to accept orders for services from NPs or non-physician providers (NPPs; as categorized by the Centers for Medicare and Medicaid Services) under Part A of Medicare. Although there is enthusiasm in Congress to get this problem fixed, projected costs and lack of a legislative vehicle have slowed progress on moving legislation to correct this problem (AANP, 2013).

Federal legislation authorizing direct Medicare reimbursement to NPs providing reimbursable Medicare services became effective January 1, 1998. Since this approval from the government, NPs have been providing reimbursable care to patients as Part B providers. Under the provisions of this law, NPs are authorized to render, order, and refer for services under their own PIN and UPIN numbers (now NPI numbers). They may order physical therapy, occupational therapy, and speech therapy; bill as consultants when providing services through telemedicine; and order and bill for performing and interpreting diagnostic tests within their scope of practice. They may also bill for services as attending physicians in the hospice care program and for services "incident to" their own service (AANP, 2013).

Medicare has recognized the autonomous practice of advanced practice registered nurses (APRNs) for nearly two decades as allowed by state law, and these healthcare professionals see the majority of patients requiring home health. Unfortunately, a quirk in Medicare law has kept APRNs from signing home-health plans of care and from certifying Medicare patients for the home-health benefit. A new requirement states that patients must see a physician or APRN in a face-to-face meeting before home health services can be authorized. Current law does allow APRNs to satisfy the face-to-face requirement, but it does not allow them to sign the final plan of care (Conant, 2013).

The bipartisan Home Health Planning and Improvement Act, H.R. 2504/S.1332, has been introduced in the Senate. The passing of this act would allow all advanced practice nurses (APNs) and PAs to sign home health orders and to meet the face-to-face requirement with Medicare. Enactment of this act will make it possible for NPs to provide necessary services for their Medicare patients by allowing them to certify patients under their care to be eligible for home care services. Passage of this legislation will reduce Medicare spending by eliminating duplicative services while also improving the quality and timelines of care to the beneficiaries (AANP, 2013).

Now that we've covered the history and current state of house calls, let's get started on the business of house calls!

Section

1

Business Basics

Chapter

1

Getting Started

⚜

"I'm convinced that about half of what separates the successful entrepreneurs from the non-successful ones is pure perseverance."

—Steve Jobs, cofounder and CEO, Apple

Six Steps to Start

1. Decide on the type of practice you will have, and a business name. When deciding on a business name, it's a good idea to have a name that's at the beginning of the alphabet so when folks start at the beginning of the house-call providers list in the yellow pages,

your name will be first. Another thing about your business name to consider is how specific it should be. I was not sure if I wanted to hire other NPs or if I would even continue to provide house calls, so I decided on a broad name. Hence, Advanced Clinical Consultants was born. You should also do a quick query in your state's business listings to see if the name you want to use already exists. You might also consider a distinctive name that is catchy, such as Speedy Housecalls, even if it isn't near the beginning of the alphabet.

Cool company names can, in and of themselves, generate media coverage, either because there's something newsworthy in the name or because many journalists are more attracted to highlight companies with fun names than boring ones. Case in point: Rent-a-Wreck (Yudkin, 2014).

2. Decide on how you will incorporate, LLC versus S-Corp. (See explanation later in this chapter.)

3. Get a TIN. (See explanation later in this chapter.)

4. Get a bank account as well as a local occupational license. Most states require healthcare professionals to have occupational licenses before setting up a company,

even if it's a home-based operation. Inquire about this specific license issue at your city hall. Additionally, you will need a bank account after you establish a name, get your TIN, and obtain your incorporation papers from your state. You will need all of these business papers to set up your bank account. The company bank account is very important because most insurance companies submit payments only electronically, through a banking institution.

5. Obtain all vital credentials and insurance numbers, as well as National Provider Identifier (NPI) and Drug Enforcement Administration (DEA) number, if applicable. After you have established your bank account, make sure you have all your necessary billing numbers for all the insurance companies that you want to participate with.

> Necessary billing numbers are all of your billing provider numbers for your newly formed business. These are your "group" or organization numbers.

Also, apply for your DEA license if you don't have one. I mention this because there may be a few times when you need to prescribe something, such as a sleep aid or an antianxiety medication.

6. Get patients and/or your bag. If you already have
   patients, all you need now is your bag. If you
   don't have patients, get some marketing materials
   (business cards and a logo, for example) and begin
   speaking with churches, home health agencies, and
   your local Council on Aging office about your new
   business. Once you have the patients, you're ready.

Types of Practices

Solo NP Practice

This is an NP-owned practice where there is only
one NP rendering care to patients. There may be another
NP or a PA/MD who provides on-call assistance, but
the sole proprietor is an NP. This is the type of practice
that I have. It was the first NP-owned house-call practice
started in the state of Louisiana.

Group Practice

This is a multi-NP practice in which multiple NPs
provide care to numerous patients throughout the life
span. One example of this type of practice is Wright &
Associates Family Healthcare in New Hampshire. It is a
very successful practice started by the multi-talented Wendy
Wright, APRN, ANP-BC, FNP-BC, FAANP, FAAN.

Concierge

This type of practice provides primary care as a cost of an annual fee. For instance, a patient may pay a healthcare provider $8,000 to have 1 annual exam, 2 follow-up (FU) exams, and unlimited prescription refills. This plan may also include 2 or 3 as needed or episodic visits for minor issues.

It is totally customizable and scalable based on what's available on the concierge company's à la carte menu.

Incorporating

You should ultimately consult your CPA or attorney to help you decide which corporation will be best for your new venture, but here are two types of incorporating that you should consider.

Limited Liability Company (LLC)

Decide if you want to establish yourself as an LLC fully knowing your risks. The LLC arose from business owners' desire to adopt a business structure that would permit them to operate like traditional partnerships. The goal was to distribute income to the partners (who reported it on their individual income tax returns) but also to protect themselves from personal liability for the business's debts, as with the corporate business form. What's nice about the LLC is that a business owner isn't responsible for the firm's debt, provided he or she didn't secure that debt personally, as with a second mortgage, with a personal credit card, or by putting personal assets on the line (Entrepreneur, 2014b).

With an LLC, the owners of the company can shield some of their assets so if the company goes under, the bank cannot take the owners' homes, cars, or personal bank accounts, for example. This is a hybrid between a full-blown corporation and a proprietorship. It is important to note, however, that if fraud is involved, a judge can perforate the full veil of LLC protection.

S Corporation (S-Corp)

An S-Corp differs from a regular corporation in that it is not a separate taxable entity from the owner. Under the Internal Revenue Code, this means that the S-Corp does not pay taxes on its net income. With an S-Corp, income and losses are passed through to shareholders and are included on their individual tax returns. As a result, there's just one level of federal tax to pay. A business must meet certain conditions to be eligible as an S-Corp. First, the corporation must have no more than 75 shareholders. Also, only the following entities may be shareholders: individuals, estates, certain trusts, certain partnerships, tax-exempt charitable organizations, and other S-Corps (but only if the other S-Corp is the sole shareholder) (Entrepreneur, 2014b).

An S-Corp must conform to a state's laws that specify how a corporation must be formed. At minimum, articles of incorporation must be filed with the Secretary of State. This particular type of organization must also file a special form with federal and state tax authorities that notifies the authorities of the election of the subchapter S status.

TIN (Tax Identification Number)

You may also hear this referred to as an EIN (employer identification number). This is the business's version of a Social Security number. It is needed immediately. You won't be able to apply for a company bank account without it. The EIN can be obtained by going to www.irs.gov and downloading the Form SS-4 or completing it online. If you decide to complete the form online, it takes only 2–3 minutes. There is no fee for either method you choose to use.

Occupational Licensing

Most states require you to have an occupational license for your business in addition to your other necessary licensing such as your professional license, DEA, and Controlled and Dangerous Substance license (CDS). If you're in a state that requires collaboration or supervision by an MD, you will also need to begin the sometimes arduous task of finding an MD collaborator, which will be addressed in Chapter 3.

Research other additional permits that may be necessary for your state jurisdictions for opening a home-based business.

Insurance

Professional Insurance

General Liability

If you have an office, general liability insurance is a must. It will cover anyone who comes in the office for slips, falls, or any accidents. In most cases, it will also cover fire, water, and interruption-of-business emergencies. This came in handy for us right after Hurricane Katrina.

If you don't have an official storefront, general liability is not necessary; however, the moment you start allowing visitors to come onto your property, begin to consider general liability insurance, or communicate with your home- owner's insurance representative about the nature of the business you are conducting in your home to see if you are covered by your homeowner's policy.

Malpractice Insurance

This is a must when you're out on your own. All healthcare providers need malpractice insurance, whether they are solo providers or work for someone else. Additionally, all insurance carriers mandate that providers have malpractice insurance before treating their beneficiaries. Some national providers are Marsh and Nurses Service Organization (NSO).

Disability Insurance

This comes in handy if you are suddenly unable to work after a traumatic accident or illness. It's not mandatory, but it's something to consider if you are a solo practice owner.

Many providers will ask me if all these additional insurances are really necessary. They want to "just start" seeing patients now. I am cautious with my answer but remain firm in that you need to protect yourself and your investments. Take the time to do this before you begin to see patients. It will be your best investment. Protect yourself before serving others.

Chapter

Getting Set up, or Setting up Your Business

❧

"I got my start by giving myself a start."

—*Madam C. J. Walker*

Business Plan

A business plan serves as something of a roadmap for how a founder will turn an idea into a full-fledged business. It typically includes information such as an executive summary, a market analysis, and financial projections. Business plans can be vital for entrepreneurs and business owners interested in lining up bank loans or attracting other stakeholders such as investors. Though a plan may change over time, entrepreneurs and owners often say that the process of mapping out how a company will operate and who its customers will be is invaluable (Entrepreneur, 2014a).

My Story: I did not fill out a business plan until several years after I started my business, but it was not to acquire a bank loan. I did it because creating the business plan is also a good exercise to give you a bird's-eye view of your financial projection several years into the future. It was nice to see all of my figures on paper instead of guessing about my financial status. In other words, a business plan is not immediately necessary unless you are looking to get bank funding; otherwise, you can complete it later. You will eventually need one as the business begins to grow and additional funding is needed.

Financing

The beauty of starting a house-call practice is that you can really start with three things: your stethoscope, a cuff, and your brain! I say this in jest, but it's true. It's nearly all I had. I had only those three things and my phone, PDA, thermometer, and school-issue pocket-sized otoscope/ophthalmoscope. You can put these items in a medical bag. bring your brain, and you're off to your first house call. When you want to begin buying other equipment and software; however, you will need financing. Unless you have about $5,000 saved, keep your day job before starting your practice. Some possible methods of financing include credit cards, bank loans, money from friends, and grants. Whatever you choose, please resist the urge to splurge. Get the positive cash flow coming in, and then spend on some equipment upgrades and phone applications.

Office Supplies and Equipment

First decide what you absolutely need and try to be as cost-efficient as possible. If you have fewer than 50 patients, an office space, which accrues overhead, as mentioned earlier, may not be needed. Get the basics: laptop; printer; Microsoft Office for Business; and a lockable, preferably fireproof, medical record cabinet if you're still using paper charts. You should also have a smartphone, as well as a wireless card for your laptop, wireless Internet capability for your phone or tablet, or a personal hotspot device. You always need connectivity.

My Story: I have great success using my iPhone as a hotspot, especially when I am in more rural areas. Of course, when I'm in assisted-living facilities, the facilities allow me to use their secure bands.

Office Space

Home Office

Many folks ask me if it's ok to start a practice in their homes. Sure, it is. The biggest issue you will face is how to handle the foot traffic. What foot traffic? Well, the more patients you acquire who are linked to a home health agency (HHA), the more HHA representatives you will have visiting to drop off and pick up orders. Plus, you will have other vendors from labs, pharmaceutical companies, hospice agencies, NP students, collaborating physicians, sitting agency owners, and more. You need to be prepared for this. You need to know how to protect your home if someone falls or has an accident on your property. Inquire with your homeowner's insurance representative. Let the insurance provider know what you are doing and the nature of your business. They are the best ones to advise you on how to be protected while running a home-based business.

Home office needs:

1. Copier/Printer/Fax/Scanner

2. Gauze, tape, bandages, and other wound-care supplies

3. Office supplies: copy paper, pens, stapler, paper clips

4. Computer (See "Computer Options" later in this chapter for more details.)

5. Desk and comfortable chair

6. Fireproof lockable file cabinet

7. A room that can be adequately secured to keep all patient data properly stored. Remember, the Health Information Portability and Accountability Act (HIPAA) requirements still exist in your home.

Traditional Office

If you venture out on your own, you will incur *overhead*. Yes, this dreaded word will now be a constant menace because you will be forever chasing it down to the lowest possible denominator. The only way to have a successful business is to bring in more money than you have overhead expenses. You won't need much more than two or three rooms to start. Look for spaces that include the cost of electricity and water with the rent. It may also help if your office is on a bus line for your employees—and for your patients, should you start seeing patients in the office.

Traditional office needs:

1. Copier/Printer/Fax/Scanner

2. Gauze, tape, bandages, and other wound-care supplies

3. Office supplies: copy paper, pens, stapler, paper clips

4. Computer (See "Computer Options" later in this chapter for more details.)

5. Desk and comfortable chair for each staff member and yourself

6. Fireproof lockable file cabinet

7. Alarm system

You will encounter other things necessary for your office that may require a monthly fee. Below is a list of a few of these items and services. Bear in mind, these additional fees increase your overhead. Some of these items are applicable in both traditional office and home office scenarios.

1. Shred Company. This is necessary if you have several bins of papers to shred daily. Do your math and look at your numbers. Hiring a shredding company for your shredding needs maybe cheaper in your region for the amount of paper work that *your* business accumulates.

My Story: I no longer need a shred company because we are 97%–98% paperless. When our small shredder box gets full, I simply take it to my local Office Depot. They weigh it and shred it for 99 cents per pound. We have found that bringing small batches to Office Depot roughly twice a month is cheaper than hiring a shredding company.

2. Medical Waste Disposal. This waste includes needles, used bandages, and/or anything contaminated by body fluids. This is necessary especially if you have a traditional office with a clinic. If you use only a few needles per week, partner with your HHAs and/or a hospital to leave your box with them. They will then discard your small needle box with their hazardous waste. This saves you a fee.

3. Computer Technician. This is necessary if you have a server in-house.

    My Story: We are a completely digital office. Everything is on a server "in the clouds." This is a plus because we rarely have an information technology (IT) issue.

4. Attorney. It's a good idea to have an attorney on retainer. You never know what will come up.

5. Security System. This is necessary for any office, whether home or traditional.

6. Website Maintenance. This is necessary if you don't manage the website yourself.

7. SFax and Dropbox. These are my two favorite document-managing systems. My life is much better because of them!

SFax is a wonderful fax-server software that allows you to visualize your faxes via encrypted secure e-mails whenever they come into your designated number. It's a nice feature, especially for those after-hours X-rays that need some attention. Pricing varies.

Dropbox is a central storage place for all documents and pictures online. My favorite part of this software is the iPhone app. I can view my documents anywhere I have Internet access and from any device. Nice. Pricing varies depending on your storage needs.

Paperless vs. Paper Medical Records

This is only a small section in this chapter because by now, most of you are already paperless or beginning to look for options to become paperless. At any rate, all medical records must be stored in a fireproof HIPAA-compliant cabinet. This is where all patient-sensitive data should be stored if you are still using paper records. If you remember to protect everything that is patient-related, you will be fine. It is also important to note that if you have accepted money from Medicare or Medicaid through the EHR (Electronic Health Record) incentive, you *must* use an electronic record instead of paper charts.

HIPAA ... stands for the Health Insurance Portability and Accountability Act, a US law designed to provide privacy standards to protect patients' medical records and other health information provided to health plans, doctors, hospitals and other health- care providers. Developed by the Department of Health and Human Services, these ... standards provide patients with access to their medical records and more control over how their personal health information is used and disclosed. They represent a uniform, federal floor of privacy protections for consumers across the country. State laws providing additional protections to consumers are not affected by this ... rule. HIPAA took effect on April 14, 2003. (MedicineNet, 2014a)

My Story: ACC uses a certified cloud-based EHR. This means we are completely paperless. Nothing patient-related is stored in our office for longer than 14 days. Once we hit a 14-day mark, all documents are taken to Office Depot for shredding. We constantly make a vigilant effort to protect privacy and to maintain HIPAA standards.

Computer Options

The first thing you must know when choosing a computer is which will work best with your current medical records, scheduling, and billing software. Another thing to consider is weight. Because you will be carrying equipment, look for a tablet or laptop that is lightweight to save your shoulder and back.

My Story: I alternate between the Surface Pro 2 tablet and the iPad. The Surface Pro 2 tablet is the best thing I have found in the form of a tablet. It has a ton of storage and is an all-around lightweight computer. The iPad is what I prefer because it is lighter than the Surface. When you're carrying all your equipment on your shoulder or backpack, you tend to look for equipment that is lightweight and portable.

I also have a 13-inch MacBook Air that I love, but it doesn't always play well with my software, so my main computer is the Surface tablet.

EQUIPMENT

The Medical Bag

Your medical bag should include, at the very least, a stethoscope, a PDA, a blood pressure cuff, a thermometer, tongue blades, a pulse oximeter, an oto/ophthalmo- scope, alcohol pads, and gloves.

You must decide early on if you want to carry or roll your equipment in a rolling medical bag. I rolled lots of equipment for years. I now carry a lightweight tote and have an additional bag with bandages, ear lavage machine, and a few other supplies stored in my car trunk. This has worked well for me because I never know what I will encounter and if I need something, it's easy to run right back to my vehicle to grab the equipment. Of course, this is all predicated on where I parked and on the neighborhood.

Additional Bag/Car Items

These are items that are not necessary to purchase now. Later, once you have a steady cash stream, you can purchase these to increase revenue. These items may not necessarily fit in your medical bag but are easily transportable in your car trunk.

1. Arterial brachial index (ABI) machine

2. Spirometry machine

3. Cerumen removal equipment

4. Needle boxes

When you're setting up your practice, there are so many decisions to be made that it can be overwhelming. If you focus on the essentials, such as: insurance, good working basic equipment (stethoscope, blood pressure cuff), and a reliable mode of transportation for the house calls, you will be off to a good start. Just start slowly with the lowest overhead you can manage, and gradually add items and equipment to your practice as you begin to have an increase in patient volume.

I've also learned that the biggest part of running a successful practice for the past ten years has been proper money management. You, as the owner, need to know how to do this or hire someone you trust to do it and do it well, or you will not be in business long. This is the focus of Chapter 4.

Chapter

3

People

❦

> *"I've learned that people will forget what you said, people will forget what you did, but people will never forget how you made them feel."*
>
> **—Maya Angelou**

Recruitment of Patients

1. Word-of-mouth is the best form of free marketing, not because it's free, but because if you're providing quality work, happy customers will spread the word.

2. Websites can drive many potential customers to your practice, especially the grown children of the potential patients (elderly). To date, second only to word of mouth, this is the highest referral source to us.

My Story: My first website was developed by me through Yahoo and hosted through Yahoo. The second website was developed by a web developer. I have found that if you want to maintain creative control (ability to change titles, add testimonials, and so on), it's easier if you develop it yourself. This worked for me because it gave me the opportunity to have complete control over my product. My current website is through Healthspot, and I absolutely love it. A team created it and my blog is hosted through Word Press. there as well. Whenever I need to change something or add a video, I simply go in through the dashboard, make the changes, and click "Publish."

It is important to remember to utilize search engine optimization (SEO) on your website for the best results.

SEO (Search Engine Optimization) "Search engine optimization is a methodology of strategies, techniques, and tactics used to increase the [number] of visitors to a website by obtaining a high-ranking placement in the search results page of a search engine (SERP) —including Google, Bing, Yahoo, and [others]. SEO helps to ensure that a site is accessible to a search engine and improves the chances that the site will be found by the search engine" (Webopedia, 2014). This means that if the name of your company is Anna Housecalls, assuming you have been search-engine optimized, whenever someone types in the name "Anna Housecalls" into Google, it will be the first business that pops up. This is important because most consumers will at least visit the website of a business that gets the first hit in their search. Ultimately, you want as many eyeballs as possible seeing your webpage. SEO will make this happen.

My Story: SEO optimization is an extra charge through our website specialist. We can have the site optimized monthly or quarterly; it all depends on how much web traffic we want driven to our site.

Obtaining a Physician Collaborator

The task of obtaining a physician collaborator in a state that requires the NP to do so can be daunting. The dilemma for most NPs can be simply finding an MD who wants to collaborate, and then there's the added difficulty of deciding on a fair price for the agreed-upon duties. I am frequently asked about the amounts that are "fair" to pay physicians for their services. The ranges I have seen are from as low as $250 per month to as high as $3000 per month. Some physicians even take a percentage of the reimbursement.

How much should you compensate? That's for you to decide, keeping the following suggestions in mind:

1. Negotiate.

2. Offer to exchange call weekends with the physician instead of paying.

3. Offer to pay the physician's malpractice insurance for working with you. (NSO insurance offers collaborator malpractice insurance, for example.)

My story: After Hurricane Katrina, it was difficult to find a collaborator—or even any doctor who had returned to the area. When I found someone, he requested that his payment be 10% of my reimbursements. Yikes! It was expensive, but I had to do it. After about a year, I found someone else, who was willing to barter for services. For instance, my physician collaborator would ask me to cover in the nursing home or to cover his weekends and holidays when he went out of town. This latter type of exchange works well because it fosters camaraderie and allows the MD to continue to see the value of having an NP on the team. Whenever you get a win-win situation, take it.

Team Members (Building Your Team)

Team /tēm/ noun: A group of people with a full set of complementary skills required to complete a task, job, or project. Team members (1) operate with a high degree of interdependence, (2) share authority and responsibility for self-management, (3) are accountable for the collective performance, and (4) work toward a common goal and shared rewards(s). A team becomes more than just a collection of people when a strong sense of mutual commitment creates synergy, thus generating performance greater than the sum of the performance of its individual members. (Web Finance, 2014)

To enhance communication and improve efficiency of care, your house calls should be coordinated with other healthcare professionals, such as hospice team members. Examples of healthcare professionals whose visits can be arranged through an HHA include a dietitian, a home health aide, an LPN, an occupational therapist (OT), a physical therapist (PT), a psychiatric nurse, an RN, a social worker (SW), a speech therapist, and a wound care nurse. Wound care can be more efficiently evaluated and managed in conjunction with a home health nurse or aide, and joint visits minimize the need for repeated dressing removals. Hospice visits can include completion of necessary controlled-substance refills to avoid delays. Home health and hospice documentation can also be completed (Unwin & Tatum, 2011).

My Story: I almost always meet a home health nurse in the home for complicated wound visits or for areas that are not safe. These visits are the best for the healthcare provider compared to all other home visits because the HHA can see your plan of care and document if there are any medication changes. This allows for seamless collaboration with all members of the home healthcare team. For complex wounds, we use a local wound facility that provides transportation for wound care. A wound care team at a local wound facility sees the patient weekly, we see the patient weekly, and the home healthcare nurse also visits weekly. Hence, the patient gets a comprehensive dressing change at least three times a week.

My team members:

1. Office Manager/Medical Assistant/Biller: Yes, she is all three of these rolled up into one person!

2. Office Administrator: She backs up the office

manager for everything, including some billing.

3. Medical Doctor(s): An MD is necessary for collaboration and an occasional house call. I have more than one collaborating MD.

4. Pharmacist: I love pharmacists who deliver meds. The pharmacist on our team delivers meds to our patients for free!

5. Social Worker: The social worker on our team is needed for all social scenarios, such as assisting with community resources and assisting with applying for additional health benefits.

6. Registered Nurse: The RN admits the patient to home health or hospice.

7. Licensed Practical Nurse: After the LPNs on our team have made visits to several of my patients during the week, they provide me with weekly follow-up calls regarding patient care, either by phone or in person.

8. Nurse Practitioner: The NP on our team works most weekends and when I take a vacation.

9. Podiatrist: Our podiatrist provides foot care in the home.

10. Physical Therapist: The PT on our team assists with gait training and endurance activities in

the home.

11. Occupational Therapist: The team's OT assists with ADLs—day-to-day living activities.

12. Home Health Agency: The HHA people are really helpful with keeping most patients out of the hospital, because they draw labs, monitor falls, and assist us with polypharmacy.

Polypharmacy can be described as the accumulation of four or more drugs by prescription or over-the-counter to be consumed. This is widely seen in the geriatric population secondary to several disease states that require medications for alleviation of pain or for blood pressure control.

13. Hospice Agency: Embracing hospice and its many benefits have greatly enhanced my house-call experience. I really enjoy hospice services because they take a lot of the day-to-day logistical stress out of dying and dealing with a terminal illness out of the hands of an already taxed family.

14. Durable Medical Equipment (DME) company: A really good and credible DME company can make life much easier. We have two DME companies that we toggle between, and things

get done more efficiently. Make sure at least one of your DME companies provides oxygen.

My Story: Not all of the people in my healthcare network, or team, work directly for me. The office administrator, manager, and NP work directly for me, but everyone else works for a separate entity or company. The healthcare professionals are all separate entities who work in harmony with the mission of my company. We help each other out and do just about anything for the vulnerable population we serve. It's a high honor to be able to serve so many with our resources.

Staffing

Staffing has probably been the hardest part of owning a business for me, second only to navigating the billing component. I often lament that if I could do everything myself, I would. Finding efficient, compassionate, and responsible staff has been a nightmare. When searching for staff, you must keep in mind that a house-call practice is a service-oriented business; thus, the people working for you should have excellent customer-service skills, particularly when dealing with patients who may not be feeling their best. I *cannot* stress enough the importance of finding the right "voice" of your office. Many people will interact with your office manager or other designated staff members before speaking with you. If the person is friendly and helpful, this will make your establishment seem professional and welcoming. In contrast, if your office personnel are not helpful or are rude, this will be a bad reflection on you and might cost you some patients.

Take the time to find qualified staff—for example, through Craig's List or your local paper. I have had success with finding staff on Craig's List, but there are a multitude of venues from which to find employees. Once you find some prospective employees, interview them and administer a simple aptitude test to ascertain their writing abilities, gauge their customer service personalities, and ascertain their grammar skills. I even have a question on the test to check if prospective employees know the difference between an NP and an MD; after all, they are looking to work for an NP.

Don't be surprised if you go through several employees over a few months until you get the right one. After 10 years in business, I can honestly say that you will know if it's a right fit in only one to two weeks. My motto is "Hire slow and fire fast."

Be sure to know the employee laws and the state laws regarding employees. For instance, Louisiana is an at-will state. This means that the employer does not need a reason to fire the employee.

Office Manager

Office managers can literally make or break the practice. Please choose wisely and hire based on experience. Do *not* assume that you will have the time to train someone on how to run your practice. Hire the right person so you won't have to fire.

You should start thinking about hiring at least a part-time office manager when you have 25 patients. The amount of paperwork and oversight necessary can be daunting, especially if you are new to the home health arena. Choosing when to take on an office manager is a personal decision because it really depends on how much you can handle, and this is something only *you* can decide. In my opinion, after 50 patients, you will need full-time help scheduling, managing, and responding to the demands of a 50-patient load, especially if all the patients have HHAs. You want to at least have someone identified before you get too busy. If you wait until business is brisk, you might be tempted to hire too fast. Be sure to hire a person who has a passion or heart for your business. The more closely this person is aligned to your mission for the business, the better, because he or she will "get" the bigger picture.

Once you have decided that you do need someone to help you, the following healthcare workers are a few examples of the types of employees you should consider adding to your practice. I utilize all of these healthcare workers in my practice right now and they are extremely helpful in making my house call practice run more smoothly.

Medical Assistants

Medical assistants provide a wide range of skills, including taking vitals, performing diagnostics, and scheduling appointments. The average salary depends on experience. The salary range is from $10 to $16 per hour.

PRN NP

PRN NPs are linked to my group Medicare/Medicaid number, and then I bill for them and negotiate a percentage for their time. I also have a staff MD collaborator who then forms a collaborating agreement with these providers. (Louisiana is a state that requires a collaborating agreement before an NP can work. This is why our collaborating MD must collaborate with the PRN NPs if they don't have their own collaborating MDs.) If the PRN NPs already have collaborating MDs, then our staff MD is not used, but we *still* link these providers (NPs) to our group number. This allows us to maintain control of all monies tied to our patients. We also have all NPs new to working with us sign a no-compete clause.

NP Students

NP students work well if they don't mind making house calls. I have had tremendous success with NP students and highly recommend them. Partner with local colleges or online universities and let them know that you are willing to have NP students shadow you.

Continue to seek out staff that believes in you and the mission and philosophy of your company. These employees will be invaluable to you. They will carry you and the practice even when you are not able to be on site or in town for emergencies. For instance, when I take trips for conferences and need my patients cared for; I depend on my collaborating physician for guidance and coverage. He is totally invested into the mission of my practice and believes in what I do. This means the world to me because he does it without pay. He asks for nothing in return. This is a fine example of someone on your team that has bought into your mission and philosophy. Most employees or team members like this often work for you expecting nothing in return. When you find wonderful team members like this; treat them well; treasure them. Send "just because" bouquets, cook meals for them, and continue show other ways to thank them because they are so hard to find.

Chapter

Once You're Established (Considerations)

❧

" Be thankful for what you have; you'll end up having more.
If you concentrate on what you don't have, you will never, ever
have enough."

—Oprah Winfrey

Money Flow

It is important to be aware of January and the inability of most patients to pay the deductible. During this time period, you must increase your volumes or seek supplemental income, depending on your payor mix (ratio of Medicare, Medicaid, and commercial insurance patients).

I used to struggle with payments and revenue every January because most of my indigent patients would not pay their deductibles for Medicare. This was an issue because when we would see the patient and attempt to bill, if the patient had not paid the $147 deductible, it would be taken from the visit that was made that day. For instance, you normally get $100 to see Ms. Nurse. It's January, and she has not yet paid her $147 deductible. You make a house call, and she tells you she does not have the money for the deductible and possibly won't be able to pay it. If you decide to provide the house call, once the claim for this visit is submitted, Medicare will see that she has not paid her deductible. The money is then captured from whatever provider she receives services from. Today, the provider is you, and you are assessed $100 of her $147 deductible. This is done to every provider she receives services from until her deductible is met. You get *zero* for the visit, and she still has a $47 remaining balance on her deductible. If you see her again for another $100 visit and she has not yet met her $47 balance, your visit will be reimbursed $53 dollars once Medicare collects her remaining deductible balance of $47. Given the aforementioned scenario, in most cases, I would not get any income in January. Not good. This was a major struggle for the practice for many, many years, until the annual wellness visit (AWV) came along. This visit and its components allowed me to breathe again in January. What's unique and lovable about the code is that it is *not* subject to a deductible. This means that in January of every year, each of my patients now gets an AWV and my revenue continues to flow. This said, once the AWV has been done and the patient has still not met his or her deductible, you're back at square 1, but the AWV does give patients time to come up with money to pay something toward the deductible. See more on AWV in Appendix 1: Billing Codes.

How Much Can You Make?

I often get asked, "How much can you make?" or "How much do you make?" This is an interesting question because when you own this type of business, you can literally make whatever you want to make. For instance, if you see 10 patients one day, you will clear roughly $400, or if you see 2 patients, you may clear only $60. (It's hard to quote because what you actually bring in depends on what level of coding has been selected or what rate you have negotiated with the payors.)

Another consideration is that you may not get paid sometimes. For example, if there are some billing errors or if there is a government freeze, your money may be placed on hold. In the case of billing errors, the payor may hold all monies until the errors have been cleared up. This is not an uncommon scenario. For example, Medicare payments are often affected by what happens in Congress, which may also hold up your desired funds. These are very real cases of money barriers; both have happened to me. Please save or have a cash flow/line of credit handy for these hair-raising times when there are delays in Congress or you encounter billing errors.

Ways to Increase Money Flow

FluFair (Flu Shot Clinic) and PneumoFairs (Pneumonia Shot Clinic) can be extremely lucrative for the organizations that host them. These are health fairs that specifically offer the influenza or pneumonia vaccine. You can host one of these health fairs and provide flu shots and/or pneumonia shots. You might even call it a vaccine fair. Make it catchy and inviting. To get the word out about your FluFairs, meet with area assisted-living facilities and offer your services as an NP. Schedule meetings at area churches and ask if you can give talks on various health topics. Just make sure to order the influenza vaccine the year before to have it on time for your event.

Billing Tip: The pneumonia vaccine is one of those once-in-a-lifetime coverage items for Medicare patients, so if the patient has received the vaccine previously but can't remember receiving it and you give it again, it will be an expense on the patient.

My Story: My very first FluFair was held at a local independent senior center. We inoculated 300 folks, monitored blood pressure, provided podiatry care, and provided gift bags to several senior citizens. (I find that it's also a good idea to team up with an optometrist, a podiatrist, an HHA, or any other vendor to enhance the services offered at a FluFair). We were able to increase the money flow to the practice by several thousand dollars from one FluFair on one day—in only four hours!

Marketing

A number of things can be considered in your marketing strategy, including promotional materials, social media, various advertisement placements, and local business groups.

Promotional material can be a tremendous asset, but it can also break the bank, so take it easy here. Order only what you need, and do so in small quantities. At www.vistaprint.com, you can find a plethora of cards, magnets, calendars, and other materials to promote your practice.

My Story: I initially ordered a batch of basic business cards (100) for $20 in a promotional special. Later, after Hurricane Katrina, I ordered some fancy cards with foil, and some waterproof mag- nets. I paid less than $100 total for 50 of each of these.

Social Media is a crucial piece of free marketing that can no longer be ignored. Every business will sooner or later learn that having a Facebook and/or Twitter account will greatly help with exposure and sales. Many patients now look for providers and correspond with their offices on social media. It takes only a few seconds to set up an account on Facebook or Twitter and is totally free!

Local magazine ads that showcase your services can drive business your way, especially if those magazines reach in your targeted population areas. For instance, if you want to do primarily geriatric house calls, then you might want to place an ad about your services in your local Council on Aging's magazine because this will be what your targeted population reads. These ads may cost from $75 to $100 per month to run.

If you use radio or television spots, try purchasing the shortest spot. These tend to be on the higher end of the cost spectrum, but you will get the most exposure here. Plan to spend about $2000–$5000 per spot, depending on your market and time spot.

Join your local Better Business Bureau, Chamber of Commerce, or Angie's List. I was surprised to hear how many folks looked at these sources as a predictor of my business value before they would let me visit their loved ones.

My Story: When I first started my practice, I had only about 100 business cards, but because of good quality care and positive word of mouth, my practice grew quickly before I even had a website, cups, or pens that advertised my company. I didn't even have a logo yet!

Billing

I could write an entire book on billing for the housecall provider! This is the most important chapter in this book because it really discusses the types of insurance plans that pay for a home visit and, more importantly, discusses the ever-popular patient "homebound" status question. "Does the patient need to be homebound before I make a home visit?" is a question that I get asked as least 10 times a week. This section answers that question.

Insurance Plans

How do you decide on an insurance company to enroll in? Enroll in all insurance companies that will allow an NP or a PA to have a panel.

> A panel can be described as the amount of patients an insurance company allows you to take care of. Some insurance companies limit NPs to a 2500 patient panel. Others don't give NPs a limit. Research them all. Some are better than others in how much they pay for a home visit and in the amount of patients they will allow you to provide care to.

Humana, Medicare, Medicaid, UnitedHealthcare, Aetna, and Cigna are just a few of the health plans that will pay for home visits. In general, I have found that most insurers will pay, but it's always best with commercial plans to call them before going to make a visit. (This is a part of eligibility and verification—see chapter 7.) Sometimes you will need a prior authorization before you make the visit. One insurance plan did not want us to make a house call because the patient did not have home health coverage. Needless to say, we could not make the house call because we would not be reimbursed by the plan and the patient could not afford to pay. She later had to have a bilateral below the knee amputation. I strongly believe that if we had been able to get in the home when we were initially contacted and to get her a timely referral to home care, this may have been avoided.

> Fee Schedule definition: A fee schedule can be described as the list of CPT codes and their respective reimbursement rates that an insurance company will pay for those designated codes.

Most insurance plans contract with NPs, but at a lower rate than the MD. For instance, most insurance companies reimburse physicians at 100% of the fee schedule for a physical examination. The NP performing the same physical examination will be paid 85% of the fee schedule rate. Please check with carriers to ascertain their rates before signing up. The rates vary widely from state to state. When you are compiling documents for insurance credentialing, it can be tedious. This is where the Council for Affordable Quality Healthcare (CAQH) comes in. The CAQH is a non- profit agency that works with various insurance companies and healthcare providers to assist with care collaboration. You sign up (www.caqh. org) and get a secure login. Then you fill out just one credentialing application that is then made accessible to various insurance companies. This service is free.

On average, the credentialing process can take 90 days or more. This period can be longer if there are errors on your enrollment application. Please be financially prepared for this delay, because you won't receive any money during this period. Most insurance companies will let you retroactively bill, but you are still not making money during this period from the house calls if you have only insurance companies as payors.

Some insurance plans want you to bill only under the collaborating physician's tax ID number. This is not optimal, but it occurs in some states. You must decide how you want to handle this barrier. Here in Louisiana, I wanted to become a Humana provider, but I was repeatedly told that for that to happen, I had to be linked with my collaborating physician. Well, this was a problem because he wanted to collaborate, but did not want to have our monies mixed. At the time, we were getting a lot of calls from Humana patients who were desirous of our services. I had to make a business decision whether it was a worthy battle to pursue, for in business, you must carefully and decidedly choose which battles to fight. I chose to continually approach my Humana representative about my practice becoming a part of Humana without being linked to the collaborator. For six months, I repeatedly called with several heartfelt stories about Humana patients who really needed our house-call services. It was enough to win; we became the first NP-owned practice in the state of Louisiana to be a Humana provider *without* being linked to a collaborator's tax ID number. This was a major success, because we could move forward as an NP practice by billing independently, which kept our monies separate from the collaborator's money. It was a worthy battle and a win for Louisiana NPs.

Does the Patient Have to Be Homebound?

As explained by AMDA (2014):

> A house call or domiciliary visit includes a history and physical exam, problem solving, and decision making at various levels depending upon a beneficiary's need and diagnosis. The patients seen may have chronic conditions and/or may be disabled either physically or mentally, making access to a traditional office visit very difficult, or may have limited support systems. The house call or domiciliary visit should lead to enhanced medical care by identification of unmet needs, coordination of treatment with appropriate referrals, and potential reduction of acute exacerbations of medical conditions, which in turn results in reduced hospitalizations and ER visits. (page 3).

According to the AMDA (2014):

> Patients must understand the nature of a prearranged visit and must consent to treatment in the home or domiciliary care facility. Coverage for this type of service is based on face-to-face time only with the beneficiary alone or with the patient/family, and the work performed during that time is documented in the chart. Travel time and related expenses are, unfortunately, not billable services and as such should not be included when determining the CPT code that best defines the service provided. Medically necessary provider visits are payable under the physician fee schedule in Medicare Part B when provided to the beneficiary in his or her private residence. (page 4).

There is no requirement that the patient must be home- bound. The reason for a visit to the home rather than in the office must be clearly documented in the visit note, as the house call is not payable or considered medically necessary if performed for the convenience of the practitioner or patient. For example, we got a call once regarding a 77-year-old female who just "didn't feel" like going to the doctor's office. We were going to suggest that she be brought into our office, but upon further discussion with her daughter, we learned that the woman had been increasingly more dyspneic and had a leg amputated. The daughter further stated that her mother's pain had increased and sometimes the prosthesis hurt. Given her mother's history and several comorbidities, we decided to see the patient in her home because of the increasingly taxing effort it was to leave her residence. The key to remember is that "medical record documentation must support a medically necessary visit and be made available to Medicare and other insurance companies upon request" (AMDA, 2014, page 3).

It is important to note that services performed for beneficiaries in residential care facilities, rest homes, or assisted living facilities are expected to occur in the beneficiary's own personal living space or in a designated space set aside for such visits. In the event of the service being performed in a designated space, such rooms are not considered a practitioner's office and shall not be used for the routine performance of rounds on beneficiaries (AMDA, 2014, page 3).

The following recommendations regarding house calls were retrieved from the AMDA (2014, page 4).

To be reimbursable by Medicare, a home or domiciliary care visit that is in lieu of an office visit, ER visit or hospital visit, must meet all of the following criteria:

- The service/visit must be medically reasonable and necessary, and the choice of the site of service must be of diagnostic or therapeutic value, not solely for the convenience of the nurse practitioner/PA/MD or patient.

- The service should be provided in a manner consistent with community standards for that service in other sites of service for similar patients, including frequency of visits, which should be consistent with the frequency for a patient with similar conditions and treatments. For example, for a beneficiary in a condition or with treatments that are commonly managed in the hospital, daily visits may be necessary.

- Services provided in the home or domiciliary setting must not unnecessarily duplicate previous services provided to the beneficiary by other practitioners, regardless of whether those practitioners provide the service in the office, facility, or home/domiciliary setting. Home/domiciliary services provided for the same diagnosis, same condition, or same episode of care as previous services provided by other practitioners, regardless of the site of service, may constitute concurrent or duplicative care.

- When such services are provided, the record must clearly document the medical necessity of said services. When documentation is lacking, the service may be considered not medically necessary.

- The house call must be ordered or personally provided by a Medicare Part B provider who is responsible for the assessment or therapy related to the service.

- The initial services provided to a patient must be either requested by the said beneficiary, his/her delegate (e.g. family or home health provider), or another Medicare provider managing the beneficiary's care. Otherwise, this action would be considered solicitation, which is illegal.

- The NP/PA/MD cannot solicit the visit.

- Visits must be scheduled prior to arrival at the facility/home, requested by a beneficiary or delegate (not solicited by the Part B provider) or substitute for a visit previously planned for the near future to that beneficiary.

- Exceptions include beneficiaries who are traveling through an area and are not residents in the location where they are being seen and beneficiaries who are being seen in their homes or domiciles for urgent or episodic illness.

- Services provided to a beneficiary by a Medicare Part B provider on the same day, as an employee of a home health agency must be of a type or quality that is beyond that available from the home health agency. Services provided during a joint visit by a Part B provider and a home health agency employee must be beyond the abilities of the home health agency staff alone and require the assistance of the home health agency employee (CMS, 2013a). Services performed to beneficiaries who are also seeing other Medicare Part B providers in their offices for the same diagnosis must add diagnostic information or therapeutic value beyond that possible in the office. This must be clearly documented in your visit notes.

- Visits to multiple beneficiaries by the same Medicare Part B provider or the same group may occur on the same date of service, but each service must meet the medical needs of the individual beneficiary. Total billing time for the sum of all the day's domiciliary beneficiary visits at one site shall not exceed the provider's time at that site. Each visit must stand on it's [sic] own, and the medical necessity of the visit must be supported in documentation.

In other words, Medicare will reimburse an NP, a PA, or an MD for a house call to a patient who is *not* homebound, but it must be clearly documented why the patient was seen in the home or living facility. Some possible reasons to see a patient in the home include cognitive and emotional inability to leave the home, home evaluation, and assessment of family resources. This whole theme of addressing the patient's homebound status will be discussed several times in this book, because it is crucial that this be understood and documented accordingly in order to have successful audits.

Reasons for Denial of Claims

The following recommendations regarding denial of claims and house calls were retrieved from the AMDA (2014, page 4).

- The record does not clearly demonstrate that the beneficiary, his/her delegate, or another clinician involved in the case sought the initial service.

- The service is provided at a frequency that exceeds that which is typically provided for similar patients in other sites of service and acceptable standards of medical practice.

- The service is solicited.

- The cumulative frequency of services across providers in all sites of service for a diagnosis exceeds acceptable standards of medical practice.

- The services are not individualized to a beneficiary's diagnoses and conditions.

- The service is provided at a frequency that exceeds that which is typically provided in an alternative site of service typical for the diagnosis, condition or treatment.

- The service is not personally performed or ordered by the rendering/billing provider.

- The service is not medically necessary and/or abnormal results will not change the beneficiary's plan of care.

A Helpful Tool for Establishing Medical Necessity
One thing that I have found helpful in establishing medical necessity is that the INHOMESSS mnemonic (impairments/immobility, nutrition, home environment, other people, medications, examination, safety, spiritual health, services) covers the components that enable me to make a more comprehesive house call (Unwin & Tatum, 2011).

Bookkeeping

It is probably best to hire a professional bookkeeper, especially if your patient base is greater than 100 clients. Bookkeepers manage and track all receipts for the practice and in most cases pay bills for the practice. Some CPA firms also perform bookkeeping duties.

A really good bookkeeper will collect all of your business receipts and tally them in software such as QuickBooks or Intuit. They will usually do this quarterly or sooner if you desire. When it's time for taxes, this person prepares your profit and loss statement and your balance sheet for the CPA. The bookkeeper can also run reports so you can see your spending patterns, which is really nice if you're on a strict budget.

Do You Need a CPA?

This is a big business decision. The CPA is a vital team member to your business. An accountant can analyze the big picture of your financial situation and offer strategic advice. An accountant produces key financial documents, such as a profit and loss statement, if needed, and files a company's taxes. After tax season is over, an accountant can also act as an outsourced chief financial officer, advising you on financial strategies, such as whether to secure a line of credit against receivables when introducing new products (Entrepreneur, 2014a).

My Story: When I first got started, I had a CPA only. This was mainly for tax purposes. After the business picked up and I had more than 100 patients, I wanted to make sure all of my receipts were properly accounted for because of the volume. This was when I hired a bookkeeper. My bookkeeper has been an invaluable asset for all of my companies. I simply download all of my files quarterly from all banking and credit cards to a secure, encrypted website, and she tallies them for me. When tax season comes, she then sends an electronic file to my CPA, and my taxes are filed accordingly.

Pay

Many new house-call business owners ask me, "Should I pay myself?" I firmly believe you should, though not everyone does. Let's look at this issue closely. If you decide *not* to pay yourself, this means that you will not contribute to local or federal taxes or to points that go toward your Medicare account; hence, when you get ready to retire, you will not have any points contributed to your Medicare. This means you should always pay yourself, even if it means that your salary will go directly back into the business. This way, you will receive points toward your retirement and pay into your business. If you pay yourself, make sure you are taking out all the appropriate taxes, including federal, state, and local, and all other necessary contributions. It is a good idea to hire a payroll processing company no matter how many employees you have, unless you want to be responsible for preparing and calculating federal taxes. Preparing the taxes and printing the checks was a little more work than I wanted to get involved with, so I have been using a payroll company from the very beginning of my business. There are several to choose from.

My Story: We have tried many payroll-processing companies and are finally satisfied with a local company. Make sure you look at the payroll company's office hours in case there is an emergency. For instance, a local company we were once using had a computer glitch so nobody got paid! I tried reaching them, but they were closed on Fridays! Needless to say, once we got the debacle resolved, we switched companies. Moral of the story: Choose a company that is open on payday!

Vacation

After you have made enough money, you might begin to think about a vacation. I often get asked if I ever take time off. My answer is always, "Yes and no," because when you own a business, you're never off even if someone is covering for you. You're the owner, and the buck stops with you.

Nonetheless, the best way to take a vacation is to ask your collaborator to take call for you, and vice versa when he or she takes a vacation. If your office is paperless, make sure the collaborating doctor has all codes and knows how to log on to your system to find patient information. We have a cloud-based electronic medical record (EMR), and it makes all the difference in the world when someone is out of town because the records are always accessible. We also occasionally utilize a PRN NP for weekends or holidays.

I always tell prospective business owners to take a vacation every year once they own their own business. If you're not able to take a few days off, take a few hours off to have some downtime. You need to recharge yourself to have more for others. How can you give to others if you're empty? That said, you, as CEO, would always be on call, even on vacation. You may have folks on call for you, but because you're the head of the company, everything flows to you: all problems, all scenarios, all checks that need to be signed. They all go through you. You may actually get to leave town and have someone take call, but if something happens, you will be notified—and I know you wouldn't have it any other way.

Section

2

The House Call

Chapter

5

The Culture of a Home

❧

"Home is where you feel at home and are treated well."

—His Holiness the 14th Dalai Lama

This is my favorite chapter of this book. I love it because I never realized how much a person's culture was tied to his or her home until I started doing house calls.

What I'd like you to take home from this chapter is how to compassionately treat others with respect and dignity in their homes when you visit, because even though you bring primary care and goodwill, you are a stranger.

Don't get into the house-calls niche if you are afraid of roaches. I visit all types of homes every day. Some of them are really nice, with butlers and maids. Others are not so nice, with roaches and other critters that make me nervous, but my care and compassion are the same in both cases. My facial expressions don't change, and my manner of happy bedside chatter is also the same. The point is, when you enter the home, you enter the patient's turf. You are no longer in control. In some of my Asian patients' homes, I must take off my shoes before entering. On these days, I make sure to wear clean socks. In some of my Southern Cajun patients' homes, I can never leave without trying fried frog legs or heavily sweetened iced tea. It is what it is. You must be prepared for whatever you are faced with and still deliver primary care with a smile on your face. This is arguably very hard when it's 110 degrees inside sweet Ms. Annie's home because she can't afford to run her AC all day, or when it's colder in your patient's home than it is outside because your patient doesn't have the money for fire logs. By the way, when I am preparing to visit a home with roaches or other visible critters, I don't bring in my medical bag. I jam all my equipment in my cargo pants and lab jacket. I am also always careful about where I sit, because if it's dimly lit, I may sit in something unidentifiable. This is not the normal occurrence, but these things will sometimes happen.

The last and most important point here is that most patients dress up for their clinic visits, so you may never know that they are living without, food, electricity, or water. If you ever make a random house call, you might be surprised at how some of your patients are living. You may find that some don't have running water or they share electricity from their neighbors. I have seen just about everything. Once you see some of the deplorable living conditions, it is sure to bring a deeper level of compassion to your heart as you care for those who may not otherwise receive health care.

Chapter

6

A Day in the Life of a Housecall Nurse Practitioner

❧

"Every day is a gift from God. There's no guarantee of tomorrow, so that tells me to see the good in this day to make the most of it."

—Joel Osteen

This chapter was written to give you an up-close and personal chance to see what is really done on a house call without being with me. Many have come to New Orleans to shadow me during The Housecall Course, but if you haven't, read this chapter very carefully.

The Housecall Course allows the learner to shadow me on the first day while making house calls throughout the New Orleans area. The second day of The Housecall Course involves a classroom experience that allows the learner to have a lively and engaging exchange of information related to house-call development and crucial business tips necessary for business development.

Following is a description of my typical day

(Displayed in military time as a nod to my former life as a Navy officer).

0500 I am awakened by Bruno Mars's "Lazy Song" or by one of my toddlers kissing my nose.

0730 I arrive at the office. (The office is a physical location away from my home. This is *quite significant* for me because I initially started in my home and worked there until Hurricane Katrina hit.) This location is approximately 1000 square feet and has four rooms: a waiting room, an exam room, an administration area, and my office. It's all we need to see some of our "not so homebound" patients who need services, such as a PAP or investigation of a mole. I sometimes bring in patients who live in really dangerous areas or patients who have homes that are literally hazardous.

0800 Now that we do our billing in-house, I review EOBs (Explanation of Benefits) and look over payor reports. During this time, my office manager on rejections, denials, and other payment issues is also debriefing me.

EOB is an abbreviation for Explanation of Benefits. Although an EOB often looks like a medical bill, the EOB actually gives you details regarding how your insurance company processed medical insurance claims. The EOB tells you what portion of a claim was paid to the healthcare provider and what portion of the payment, if any, you are responsible for (Elmblad, 2014).

0830 I make sure my bag is restocked with hand sanitizer, otoscope tips, gauze, gloves, and anything I used the day before that needs to be replaced.

I have medical assistants (MAs) working for me. One of them is the office manager and handles the financial matters. The other MA is more of an administrator; she is the one who, around this time, is calling the patients with appointments for the day to verify that they will be home, as well as double-checking any last-minute address or phone number issues. For instance, we call each person the night before and sometimes don't get confirmations that everyone will be home. This MA follows up on those missed calls to confirm the visit or to select another person within a five-mile radius for me to see. I see only patients who are within a five-mile radius within a day. That is, I usually see six to eight patients all within a certain zip code and within five miles of each other on the same day. This cuts down on gas and makes the process really efficient.

0900 Patients are confirmed. They are mapped on my phone GPS app, and I leave.

0910 I stop for gas.

0930 I arrive at the home of Ms. Blu Bayou, my first case of the day.

This is my second favorite section of this book because it describes the lives of a few of my actual patients who are typical of the people I meet in a given day. Of course, all names have been changed and some features altered to maintain anonymity. These represent a small snippet of the lives you can touch through house calls.

Ms. Bayou is 101-years-old. She has hypothyroidism, osteoarthritis, and GERD. She has been a patient of the practice for 5 years. She walks 5 feet and desats to 88% on RA. Her 92-year-old brother cares for her. They don't have a car and live in a small shot- gun house near the bayou. She has sitters from a personal care agency and receives skilled nursing and PT from home health. She takes no meds because they are "evil." The only thing that she needs is castor oil and a little bit of coconut oil to keep everything working. She has a cup of tea with a dash of vinegar every morning. She is homebound because of her compromised oxygen levels and overall frailty secondary to her chronic disease states. All of her meds are delivered by a local pharmacy, as is the case for most of the patients who are homebound.

0950 I leave the home of my first patient, Ms. Bayou. **1000** I arrive at the home of my second patient, Mr. Satchmo.

Mr. Satchmo is 78-years-old. He has glaucoma, which is worsening, prostate cancer, and COPD. He is relatively new to the practice. He still drives and enjoys an occasional Cuban cigar. He learned of our practice from an Internet search for "home docs." He lives in a duplex. His elderly sister lives next door. She is 88-years-old and still works at a local library. She also drives. Mr. Satchmo has a regular

PCP but wants to have a provider to visit him on the days when he seems more "winded." Whenever he is seen, all documents are forwarded to his current PCP. He picks up his meds when he goes to the adult day care. He is not necessarily homebound, but when he has an exacerbation of COPD, I provide a house call and an ER visit is avoided.

1045 I leave the home of Mr. Satchmo, my second patient for the day.

1100 I arrive at the home of my third patient, Ms. Saint.

Ms. Saint is probably the most colorful personality I will ever meet. She is 82-years-old and still works as an RN at the local blood bank. She calls herself a modern-day vampire with benefits. She has schizophrenia, IBS, dementia, and diabetes. She never takes her medications the right way but manages to keep her A1C below 6. "It's the cinnamon, bay-bee," she says in a deep Southern accent. She has been a patient of the practice for eight years and says she will never leave. Like Mr. Satchmo, she has a regular PCP but calls our house-call service when she is too weak to leave her home. Last week, we were called over for an urgent call because she somehow got a piece of pinecone lodged in her foot and could not see how to get it out. We treated her in her home, and she thus avoided an ER visit.

1145 I leave the home.

1200 I have lunch.

This is where things get tricky. I always strive to eat healthy when I'm mobile—emphasis on the word *healthy*. Truth be told, it's a process. I either pack my lunch the night before or strategically plan to be completely done with patient visits by lunchtime to go home and eat a healthy meal. I can also purchase healthier fast-food options, but it's hard to eat a salad while driving—a burrito, now, well… You get the picture. Most days, I go for taking lunch in an insulated lunch bag. This way, I know exactly what I'm getting. A typical meal will be a smattering of almonds, dried fruit, a protein bar, and a peanut butter and jelly (PBJ) sandwich. I also always carry water. Always.

PBJ sandwiches are my favorite because they are not as sensitive to heat such as a tuna salad or any other mayo-based sandwich.

1300 I have cut the day short to head back to the office for a billing webinar on the new ICD-10 coding.

1400 I finish charting and return phone calls.

1500 I'm done for the day. I always try to be done by 1500. This gives me time to spend with the babies.

Chapter

7

Eligibility and Verification

❧

"Lost time is never found again."

—Benjamin Franklin

Checking patient insurance eligibility comes first, before any home visit is made. It is crucial because in home health, time is money. If you don't check a patient's insurance eligibility before a house call is made and they no longer have an insurance plan that you are credentialed with, you will not be reimbursed for visiting the patient. This is lost revenue. This is lost time. When patients present to a traditional office for service, they are immediately asked for identification and insurance cards. Well, with house calls, this can be a little tricky because sometimes the info may not actually come from the patient but from a family member, hospital administrator, or social worker.

The important thing to remember when verifying coverage status is to make sure that HIPAA practices are followed when patient information exchange occurs. For instance, never take patient information via a text message or e-mail. Sometimes, referrals come fast and someone will want to e-mail you. Please don't accept this. Tell the person to fax the information or to send it through a certified encrypted EHR.

Eligibility can be assessed or verified in a few ways. The first option is through your EHR, however. This is a feature most often included with your Practice Management (PM) component, but some vendors allow you to purchase it without purchasing the PM portion if you are interested in only the EHR as a stand alone item. The next option is via a website called Navinet (www. navinet.net). It's free, depending on what insurances you are accessing through the site. We used Navinet for a few years, until we decided to purchase eligibility verification through our PM software. Lastly, you can use CortexEDI (www.medicareeligibility.com). I have also used this one in the past. The prices are worthwhile; depending on the volume you are checking each month.

Verification of the patient's information occurs when you assess the patient's information from any of the aforementioned avenues for a copayment or deductible. Medicare deductibles are due annually, and copayments are due after every visit or service rendered. It's important to note that care plan oversights (see Chapter 14) are susceptible to copayments.

My Story: We currently check eligibility via the PM component of our EHR (HealthFusion). It is cloud- based and able to be used efficiently on any Apple or Android device without issues. We also do our billing through HealthFusion. It is a complete stop for us, making things simpler and allowing for faster healthcare delivery to large volumes of patients in multiple facilities and homes.

Once patient insurance eligibility and verification have been confirmed, then comes confirmation that the patient will be home—"patient-home" confirmation (discussed in the next chapter). All these steps are crucial because you don't want to lose money visiting a patient who is no longer on your plan, or lose time by visiting a patient who is not home. Lost time is truly never found again. Lost time *is* lost money in the house-calls business.

Chapter

8

Confirmation, Safety, and What to Wear

❧

> *"Is there anything more annoyingly creepy than an unspoken dress code?"*
>
> —*Douglas Coupland*

Confirmation

Patient Home confirmation involves speaking with someone *before* the house call. This conversation is necessary to confirm that the patient will be home and to reconfirm the address where the house call will occur. After the schedule is established, I plot all my visits according to a five-mile geographic location using *MapQuest* or a GPS app on my phone. (This is just one way of many ways to schedule your day. You want to be as efficient as possible.)

Safety

I always tell medical practitioners new to the field of house calls to be extra vigilant, especially in areas that are unfamiliar. In the end, I have a few simple rules:

- Don't talk on the phone or text on the way between the car and home.

- Keep driving if *anything* looks or feels "off." I am notorious for doing a "drive-by" if someone I don't recognize is sitting on the porch. In these cases, I simply tell the patient that I will reschedule, and then I go back when the coast is clear.

- Change your routine. For instance, don't see the same patient every Wednesday at 0800. It's always best to give a time range (9–11, for example), anyway.

- Always keep your car gassed up.

- Ladies, never get on an elevator with a strange

man or several men. Use your gut instincts and the type of building you are in for clues as to what to do.

- If you travel to more urban, "hood" areas, go early, and always call the patients when you are about five minutes away. You want them looking for you.

- When entering a home, always know the exits and be looking for additional ways to exit if something happens. On habit, any time I enter a home, I immediately begin looking at how many locks are on the doors, at the latches on the windows, at the shutters, alarm systems, security cam- eras, window screens (window screens can be a barrier in case you need to jump out of the window to escape, it's best to size these things up early on), and fire escapes. It's now second nature.

- Ask that pets be caged if they are large or pesky. The last thing you need is to get bitten.

- Try not to keep your bag too heavy. If you need to run from dogs or people, you need to be light on your feet.

- Check in with the office often when you're out on the road. I often call the office to let them know where I am. I do this between all patients or at least after every other patient. This allows your staff to know your whereabouts and also enables you to receive any updates or patient changes that may have occurred for the patients that you are headed to visit.

Folks always tell me to carry mace. It's somewhere in my bag, but I'm too clumsy to even use it. I figure I would probably spray myself, so, for me, it's best to be hypervigilant, to blend in, and to not let texting or talking on the phone be a distraction to my safety.

What to Wear

I am frequently asked about what is appropriate attire for house calls. Of course, I love bulleted lists, so please see below recommendations:

- Wear closed-in shoes. This is necessary because you never know what you will encounter in someone's home, especially if you are walking in dimly lit areas.

- I prefer scrubs, but usually the dressier kind that can easily flow into a pharmaceutical dinner pro- gram after work.

- I usually wear a lab coat that is any color but white, or I will wear a light windbreaker-type jacket with the company logo on it.

- Always wear your name tag or company badge. This makes you look professional and adds credibility.

- Always wear attire with your company's logo when possible. This is constant advertising for your company. I can't tell you how many people look at my company logo on my clothes and ask, "Where are you all located?" or "What kind of business is that?" This is free marketing.

- Wear scrubs or casual street clothes. Assess your neighborhood to see what you should wear. For instance, when I'm going to a more urban area, I wear casual-looking scrubs with a matching top. When I go to a more affluent area, I wear more business casual attire. The idea is to blend in with the clientele you are providing care to.

To conclude, when you make a home visit or house call, you want to be as professional as possible in both action and dress, but not overly dressed as you might be in a traditional office setting. Use every opportunity to show your company brand, too. I get so many questions about my logo and what it means. It's always a time to promote and educate the public about the wonderful field of house calls.

Chapter

9

Typical House Call Procedures and Codes

❧

"You have to learn the rules of the game. And then you have to play better than anyone else."

—Albert Einstein

Billing and coding are the two rule masters in the house-calls arena. The sooner you learn all there is to know about them, the better off you and your practice will be. As you may have noticed already, I have broken the topic of billing up and scattered it about this book because it's a dense subject that we all love to hate but desperately need for continued success.

Procedural Coding

These codes can be used on home health patients, hospice patients, or on any other patient who is seen in the home or in an assisted-living facility by an NP/PA/MD or anyone else allowed to bill for evaluation & management (E&M) services.

All of the following coding information was retrieved from CMS (2013) Physician Fee Schedule search feature.

69210 and G0268: These include performance of the procedure for one or both ears and should be billed only once per visit. Bill 69210 for medically reasonable and necessary removal of impacted cerumen requiring a physician's skill. Bill G0268 only where physician's skill is needed to remove impacted cerumen on the same day as audiologic function testing performed by his/her employed audiologist. If the audiologist removes the cerumen, he/she cannot bill HCPCS code G0268 or CPT code 69210. In such case, cerumen removal does not require a physician's skill and is considered to be included in the payment for the audiologic testing.

Cerumen Removal: Welch Allyn Ear Lavage System or metal syringe. Code: 69210. Reimbursement: $40.

Foreign Body Removal from Ear: Welch Allyn Ear Lavage System or metal syringe. Code: 69200 Reimbursement: $40.

HCPCS code G0268 must be billed on the same claim as the audiologic function test(s) done. This code is also subject to the multiple surgery rules when billed with other surgical procedure(s) done on the same date of service. The same physician may bill an E&M service on the same day as 69210 or G0268 only if documentation supports it to be a significant separately identifiable service on the same day as the procedure. In such cases, modifier-25 should be added to the E&M code. CMS will consider payment for both an E&M visit and the cerumen removal only when all the following criteria are met: the nature of the E&M visit is for anything other than the removal of cerumen; during an unrelated patient encounter, the physician observes impacted cerumen or the patient lodges a specific complaint about his/her ear during the encounter; otoscopic examination of the tympanic membrane is not possible due to the impaction; removal of the impacted cerumen requires the expertise of the physician or non-physician practitioner and is personally performed by them; and the procedure requires a significant amount of time and effort and all of the above criteria are clearly documented in the patient's medical record.

Additional Home Procedures

ABI Machine: Ankle Brachial Index. Code: 93922. Reimbursement: $100–$125 per study.

Spirometry: Pulmonary Function Testing. Code: 94010. Reimbursement: $30–$40 per study.

Chapter

10

Forms 485 and 487s, and Telephone Orders

❦

"If you don't like how things are, change it! You're not a tree."

—*Jim Rohn*

I f you will be working with HHAs or hospice agencies, this is an important chapter for you. These are very important documents that are necessary for the HHAs to provide home care to your patient and require your physician's signature (if applicable).

CMS Form 485

The Form 485/CMS485 is also known as the Plan of Care. A 485 is a form that must be signed by the physician for the HHA to provide care and to bill Medicare. This is the form that initiates a patient's care or restarts the care after a hospitalization. An NP or PA cannot sign this plan of care.

Telephone Orders

Telephone orders also cannot be signed by NPs. This means that you will need to figure out the system that best works for you and your collaborator to get the physician signature. What we currently do is have the collaborator sign the 485s and orders when he comes to the clinic, or I will personally deliver them to his office for a signature. This is a win-win situation because I often use this time to discuss complex patients with him.

CMS Form 487

A Form 487 is a form that must be signed by a physician for the HHA to document new orders not covered on the 485. As with the 485, an NP/PA cannot sign the form 487.

As noted above, NPs and PAs are not yet able to sign HHA orders, 485s, or 487s. You may hear that NPs and PAs can at least sign the orders, but this is not true.

There are not yet any successfully passed federal or state laws or regulations allowing these healthcare providers to sign orders or 485s and 487s yet, though there are bills awaiting approval on this hot issue. I believe the NP profession is doing everything possible to lobby for a change in this area and that it's only a matter of time before the bill will be successfully passed.

Chapter

11

Emergency Care

❧

"Always turn a negative situation into a posi- tive situation."

—Michael Jordan

The goal of primary care based in the home is to keep the patient out of the ER. In my practice, we treat only chronic diseases, and we encourage our patients to call 911 for all emergency situations such as chest pain, increased dyspnea, and other life-threatening scenarios. They also are advised to call our practice once they are discharged from the hospital. I usually follow up with a house call within seven days after a hospital discharge.

There are several diagnostic options for maintaining your patient in the home. One very useful tool is the portable x-ray. If you do careful research in your area, you may discover that a number of local companies offer this invaluable service that keeps your patient from having to go to the ER for a simple chest x-ray. Today's portable digital x-ray machine can take advantage of the latest innovations in medical imaging technology—which, as you know, has shrunk not only in physical size but also in cost—while providing more capabilities and versatility than ever. Digital technology means that modern portable x-ray machines require no film and no developing, thanks to DICOM (Digital Imaging and Communications in Medicine).

DICOM is an application layer for the transmission of medical images, waveforms and accompanying information. The National Electrical Manufacturers Association (NEMA) originally developed DICOM and the American College of Radiology for computerized axial tomography (CAT) and magnetic resonance imaging (MRI) scan images. It is now controlled by the DICOM Standards Committee and supports a wide range of medical images across the fields of radiology, cardiology, pathology and dentistry. (Rouse, 2011)

The images taken with a portable digital x-ray machine are saved in a format that is fully compatible with the latest DICOM protocols and "can easily be transferred to any PC equipped with DICOM software and [then] stored, e-mailed, archived and/or enhanced" (Blocker, 2010).

My Story: Often, an HHA nurse or assisted-living facility nurse will call me about a patient who sounds bad respiratory-wise but is afebrile. I instinctively order a chest x-ray to see what may be going on in the lungs. I have caught many pleural effusions, or pneumonias, and have saved the patients visits to the ER with prompt medical interventions.

Always, my goal is to keep the patient out of the ER, and mobile radiology is often the sole diagnostic tool that I turn to aid in my diagnosis decision.

Chapter

After-Hours Calls and Care

❧

"To be trusted is a greater compliment than being loved."

—George MacDonald

It is a good idea to have a *live* telephone answering service to answer your calls or to have a voice mail clearly stating your office hours as well as what the patient is to do if an emergency has occurred outside of regular office hours. Most insurance companies require this now. I have had success with a program called Ring-

A-Doc. It is an answering service in which the patient can leave a message. If it's urgent, the patient presses a button to indicate that, and then on-call provider (me) is immediately paged by the iPhone app. I like it, but we are researching to make sure it is compliant for our new health plans. The price is excellent at $50 per month, compared to more than $150 per month charged by traditional answering service vendors.

My Story: A lot of my patients have my cell phone number. That's right, they have my direct number. I realize this is giving the family a certain measure of trust by allowing them to have my cell number. The funny thing is, they rarely use it. Oddly enough, clinicians call me more! When patients and their families know they have complete access to you, they consider this an honor and typically will not abuse it.

Chapter

13

Insurance Company Contracting

❧

"Nothing is impossible; the word itself says 'I'm possible!'"

—*Audrey Hepburn*

There are several insurance companies to choose from. Some are more professionally friendly to NPs than others are, meaning some insurance companies will not allow NPs on their plan unless the NP is linked with an MD. Others will suggest that they pay NPs at least 30% less than Medicare pays an NPP. In light of this, please be prepared to request otherwise and to fight for your rights and the services of your patients. For example, when I first returned to New Orleans after Hurricane Katrina, I was not allowed on a certain insurance plan, despite the fact that no other provider in the area was available to make house calls. I wrote letters and called for a few months and was eventually allowed on the plan. The plan's administrator later told me that no NP or PA in the state of Louisiana had ever asked to be on the plan before I had.

Please don't be afraid to get credentialed on every plan that allows NPs and PAs. Plus, consider including pursuit of the insurance companies that won't allow NPs to have a panel. It's a pioneering feat to seek out the companies that are not considering nurse practitioners to be included or considered for a patient panel. If you win a company that has not included NPs in the past, it would be a monumental triumph for the profession and a win for your company that is for sure to garner bragging rights. You maybe surprised at what a little persistence will do. After all, nothing is impossible. Be unstoppable and persistent about the promotion of your profession.

Chapter

14

Defensive Charting
and Billing

❧

"The way to get started is to quit talking and begin doing."

—Walt Disney

Billing and processing of claims form the nucleus of any medical practice. If you or your designated biller fails here, nobody eats. It's a tough area to master, but every healthcare provider should learn the intricacies of billing. I mean that you should learn by doing in this instance. This is something you must do, because at the end of the day, the medical provider, not the biller, has the provider number.

Defensive Charting

If you provide a house call to a Medicare beneficiary, you must show that the patient has considerable difficulty leaving the home and that this is why you provided a house call in lieu of the patient going for a traditional provider visit. The following statement is provided for all of my visits to a home:

Patient was seen today in his/her own environment because in my professional opinion the risks to the patient's health of an office visit far outweigh the benefits, and the home visit is therefore medically necessary in lieu of an office visit or other outpatient venue.

Once you have mastered the defensive charting method, it's time for billing and processing of your claims from said charting.

Billing

Before you or your billing company begins to process claims, you need to have all the insurance plan provider numbers for Medicare, Medicaid, and the companies you plan to bill set up with your biller. You will need an NPI for yourself, as well as a group NPI for the business even if you will be a solo provider. The NPI is a unique identification number for covered healthcare providers (both individuals and groups). Covered healthcare providers and all health plans and healthcare clearinghouses must use the NPIs in the administrative and financial transactions adopted under HIPAA. According to CMS (2012, p. 2), "The NPI is a 10-position, intelligence-free numeric identifier (10-digit number). This means that the numbers do not carry other information about healthcare providers, such as the state in which they live or their medical specialty. The NPI must be used in lieu of legacy provider identifiers in the HIPAA standards transactions."

As I noted, you will need your own (individual) NPI and another *separate* NPI for your group before you begin billing. For example, Sally, an NP, is starting her own practice, Housecalls on the Dock. Sally will have her own NPI as an NP and then will apply for a group NPI for Housecalls on the Dock. Once she has obtained the group NPI, it is then used on all the Medicare enrollment forms to obtain a group provider number.

If you're outsourcing the billing, expect to pay somewhere in the range of 5%–10% of your reimbursements from the insurance companies. It's not cheap, but a bad biller will sink your profits, get you audited, or close your doors. Choose wisely. Get references and research billers thoroughly before signing a contract. From a good billing company, you should receive monthly reports on your financial statistics. If you don't get this, ask for it.

We have outsourced the billing for the past 10 years, but have very recently moved the billing in-house, doing it ourselves to save all those billing fees that would normally be paid to an outside billing company. Billing and looking at the profitability of your practice regarding what you can afford is a delicate balance. We researched many electronic medical record systems that had a billing component to it. Most EHRs come stand-alone or with the billing component combined as one unit, which is sometimes called the Practice Management feature. Some companies offer a free EHR, but want 5%–7% of the profits in exchange for the free use of their product. In these cases, if we did not have monthly reimbursements of at least $1,500–$75,000, we would have been assessed an automatic monthly fee of $600–$1,500, depending on the system. Last, a few EHRs allow you to forego using their billing services, but then you pay for the monthly subscription ranging from $500–$1,200 per month.

The best advice I can give is for you to take your

time and find the right solution for you. Keep in mind that there is no perfect system. Don't be fooled by the salespeople.

If you can, take a few billing and coding courses. With all the new laws regarding ICD-10, you need to be knowledgeable about what your biller is doing. After all, as the auditors told me, "The onus for billing and coding is on the provider because you have the number, *not* the biller." It's chilling but true. Learn by doing.

Care Plan Oversight

The following was retrieved from CMS (2014).

Care plan oversight (CPO) is the physician supervision of a patient receiving complex and/or multidisciplinary care as part of Medicare-covered services provided by a participating home health agency or Medicare approved hospice. CPO services require complex or multidisciplinary care modalities involving:

- Regular physician development and/or revision of care plans;

- Review of subsequent reports of patient status;

- Review of related laboratory and other studies;

- Communication with other health professionals not employed in the same practice who are involved in the patient's care;

- Integration of new information into the medical treatment plan; and/or adjustment of medical therapy.

The CPO services require recurrent physician supervision of a patient involving 30 or more minutes of the physician's time per month. Services not countable toward the 30-minute threshold that must be provided in order to bill for CPO include but are not limited to:

- Time associated with discussions with the patient, or with his or her family or friends, to adjust medication or treatment;

- Time spent by staff getting or filing charts;

- Travel time; and/or

- Physician's time spent telephoning prescriptions in to the pharmacist unless the telephone conversation involves discussions of pharmaceutical therapies.

Implicit in the concept of CPO is the expectation that the physician has coordinated an aspect of the patient's care with the HHA or hospice during the month for which CPO services were billed. The physician who bills for CPO must be the same physician who signs the plan of care.

NPs, PAs, and clinical nurse specialists (CNSs), practicing within the scope of State law, may bill for care plan oversight. Non- physician practitioners must have been providing ongoing care for the beneficiary through evaluation and management services. These non-physician practitioners may not bill for CPO if they have been involved only with the delivery of the Medicare-covered home health or hospice service.

Home Health

CPO G0181

The following coding information is from CMS (2013a).

Non-physician practitioners (NPPs—i.e., NPs and PAs) can perform CPO only if the physician signing the plan of care provides regular ongoing care under the same plan of care as does the NPP billing for CPO and either:

- The physician and NPP are part of the same group practice; or

- If the NPP is an NP or CNS, the physician signing the plan of care also has a collaborative agreement with the NPP; or

- If the NPP is a PA; the physician signing the plan of care is also the physician who provides general supervision of physician assistant services for the practice.

Billing may be made for CPO services furnished by an NPP when:

- The NPP providing the CPO has seen and examined the patient;

- The NPP providing CPO is not functioning as a consultant whose participation is limited to a single medical condition rather than multidisciplinary coordination of care; and

- The NPP providing CPO integrates his or her care with that of the physician who signed the plan of care (CMS, 2013a).

NPPs may not certify the beneficiary for home health care.

Certification (G0180) and Recertification (G0179) of Home Health Services

According to CMS (2013a):

G0180 is used to report physician services for an initial certification of Medicare-covered home health services. This code is used when the patient has not received Medicare- covered services for at least 60 days.

G0179 is used to report physician services for re-certification of Medicare-covered home health services. This code is used after a patient has received services for at least 60 days (or one certification period) when the physician signs the certification after the initial certification period. HCPCS code G0179 will be reported only once every 60 days, except in the rare situation when the patient starts a new episode before 60 days elapses and requires a new plan of care to start a new episode.

An ordering physician need not have a face-to-face encounter (F2F) with the patient to bill for these services if the collaborating NP is visiting the patient. The collaborating MD, however, still must sign the F2F form. I actually sign the F2F and then have my collaborating MD cosign it. All home health physicians' orders and subsequent home health verbal orders must be signed by the collaborating physician prior to an HHA billing Medicare.

What Physician Services Are Included in These Codes?

Services that fall into these categories could include the following:

- verification that the HHA complies with the physician's plan of care; and

- a physician may not count certification/ re-certification time toward the 30-minute monthly CPO minimum.

Who Can Bill for these Codes?

These codes have been restricted to physicians who

are authorized to order/certify that home health services are required. HHAs may not bill these physician codes. The following physicians may order Medicare home health services:

1. Medical Doctor

2. Podiatrist

3. Osteopath

4. Psychiatrist

PAs, NPs, and chiropractors may not sign orders for Medicare-covered home health services and therefore may not bill using these physician codes for certification or re-certification.

Hospice

CPO G0182 with GV modifier according to CMS (2013a)

The attending physician (or the NP who has been designated as the attending physician) may bill for hospice CPO when acting as an attending physician. An attending physician is one who has been identified by the individual, at the time when he or she elects hospice coverage, as having the most significant role in the determination and delivery of his or her medical care. The designated attending physician is not employed by or paid by the hospice. The CPO services are billed using

Form CMS-1500 or electronic equivalent.

Under the Final Physician Fee Schedule Rule, published in the Federal Register in 2009, NPs, PAs, and CNSs, practicing within the scope of state law, may bill for CPO.

NPPs are allowed to bill for physician home health CPO even though NPPs cannot (1) certify a patient for home health services and (2) sign the plan of care.

For beneficiaries who have elected the hospice benefit, physicians or NPPs who have been identified by a beneficiary to be his or her attending physician may submit claims for CPO.

> For physicians or NPs who are employed by a hospice agency, CPO is not separately payable because the MD is being paid directly by the hospice agency.

Additional issues to consider regarding CPO billing follow:

- Pay for NP/PA/MD home health plan CPO services (HCPCS code G0181) is no more than once per calendar month per patient and is, on average, $65 per patient per month;

- Pay for NP/PA/MD hospice CPO services (HCPCS code G0182 with GV modifier) when billed by an NP is, on average, $100 per patient per month;

- Pay for NP/PA/MD hospice CPO services under HCPCS code G0182 is no more than once per calendar month per patient. Payment average $60- 80 per month.

Incident-To Billing for the NP and PA

"Incident to" billing refers to the provider billing of services and supplies that are performed by auxiliary personnel. Medicare defines a medical provider as including NPs, CNSs, certified nurse midwives, MDs, PAs, clinical psychologists, clinical social workers, and PTs and OTs. The medical provider must first see the patient and develop a plan of care and initiate the course of treatment. The incident-to service provided by the auxiliary personnel is then an incidental part of the patient's treatment. The patient can see the auxiliary personnel for continued treatment of the initial problem that was presented to the provider (NP/PA/MD).

If the auxiliary personnel discover a new problem at a visit, the patient must be referred back to the provider for evaluation and development of a new plan of care and a new treatment plan. The medical provider must demonstrate an active participation in the ongoing care of the patient, such as providing services regularly that reflect participation on an ongoing basis. Reimbursement is based on 100% of the provider's fee schedule amount (Reimbursement Task Force, 2012).

Another consideration under the Medicare incident-to provision is to allow services provided by an NPP to be reimbursed at 100% of the physician fee schedule by billing under the physician's name and NPI. There may be some practice settings in which the NPP, such as an APRN, would therefore bill incident-to to increase the reimbursement from 85% to 100% of the physician's fee schedule.

Certain requirements need to be meet before billing incident-to:

1. The services must be an integral, although incidental, part of the provider's professional service.

2. The services are of a type commonly furnished in providers' offices or clinics.

3. The services are furnished under the provider's direct personal supervision and are furnished by the provider or by an individual who is an employee or independent contractor of the provider. Direct supervision does not require the provider's presence in the same room, but the provider must be immediately available.

4. The provider must perform all initial home visits and subsequent visits with a frequency that reflects their proposed treatment plan (CMS, 2013a).

5. The provider under whose name and number the bill is submitted must be the individual present in the office suite when the service is provided.

6. The documentation in the patient chart must match the service that was billed.

Incident-to services may be covered in some medically underserved areas where there are only a few providers available to provide services over broad geographic areas or to a large patient population. The lack of medical personnel (and, in many instances, an HHA servicing the area) significantly reduces the availability of certain medical services to homebound patients. Some physicians and physician-directed clinics therefore call upon nurses and other paramedical personnel to provide these services under general (rather than direct) supervision. In some areas, such practice has tended to become the accepted method of delivery of these services. For the medically underserved scenarios, the following criteria must still be met:

1. The patient must be homebound. This is not necessarily bedridden, but absences from the home are infrequent, usually for the purposes

of receiving medical treatment, and there exists a normal inability to leave home, and to do so would present a daunting or taxing effort.

2. The service is an integral part of the provider's service to the patient and is performed under general provider supervision by employees of the provider or clinic. General supervision does not require the provider to be physically present when the service is performed. The auxiliary personal immediately contacts the provider if additional care guidance is needed (CMS, 2013a).

3. Coverage will not be considered if there is a participating home healthcare agency that could provide the needed services on a timely basis.

An abundance of services are allowed to be performed under the general supervision of a provider by a house-call provider, including injections, venipuncture, EKGs, therapeutic exercises, insertion and sterile irrigation of a catheter, changing of catheters and collection of catheterized specimen for urinalysis, dressing changes, replacement and/or insertion of nasogastric tubes, and removal of fecal impaction (including with enemas), just to name a few (CMS, 2012).

For additional billing codes, please see Appendix I.

Chapter

15

Audits

❦

"Winners make a habit of manufacturing their own positive expectations in advance of the event."

—Brian Tracy

I remember getting the envelope from Advanced Medical requesting more than 20 charts. Advanced Medical is a contracted agency with Medicare to perform audits on healthcare providers. It is just one of many such agencies. My heart sank because I did not know what to do; at the time, I didn't know what it meant to receive a request for records. Little did I know, a nightmare was on the horizon. We were audited for the period immediately following Hurricane Katrina. I was crestfallen at the idea of being audited, but I swiftly realized that I had to hastily locate a lot of data that had been permanently lost. I made a call to the vendor to explain my plight. The missing charts from Katrina were subtracted and replaced with more.

I initially completed my own responses through the first two phases but later retained a local law firm to handle the last phases. It was a long process that was stretched over three awful years, but in the end, we were victorious. If we had lost, we would have had to pay back hundreds of thousands of dollars. Throughout the experience, I remained positive and envisioned victory even though I was severely stressed and emotional. I believe this positive frame of mind helped me, along with a wealth of daily prayers for strength.

Audit Tips Maintain Proper Documentation of Homebound Status

Per CMS (2013b):

Under the home health benefit (Medicare Part A), the beneficiary must be confined to the home for services to be covered. For home services provided by a house-call practitioner using these codes, the beneficiary does not need to be confined to the home. The medical record must document the medical necessity of the home visit made in lieu of an office or outpatient visit.

The visit will be regarded as a visit of convenience unless the medical record clearly documents the necessity for each visit.

Follow All Documentation Requirements

The CMS (2013b) further states:

In support of [the medical record clearly documenting the necessity for each home visit], the documentation of each beneficiary encounter must include at a minimum:

- Reason for the encounter and relevant history;

- Physical examination findings, and prior diagnostic test results, if applicable;

- Assessment, clinical impression, or diagnosis; and

- Medical plan of care.

Thus, a payable diagnosis alone does not support the medical necessity of *any* service. All documentation must be available to Medicare, Medicaid, and other commercial insurance carriers upon request.

Have in Place Utilization Strategies

According to the AMDA (2014):

It is expected that house-call visits will be performed as indicated by current medical literature and/or standards of practice. The frequency of visits should be consistent with the frequency at any other site of service for that code. The fact that there is the overwhelming presence of inactive or chronic conditions does not constitute medical necessity for any setting. There must always be a chief complaint documented or a specific reasonable and medically necessary need for each home visit (AMDA, 2014).

It is important to know that even if you have all of your documentation accurately recorded, you will still be audited. As long as you are caring for insurance company beneficiaries, the companies have a right to monitor your charting to ascertain the level of care their patients are receiving. Continue to ask yourself the hard questions before you visit a patient in his or her home. Some of these include but are not limited to:

- Does this person see other providers in a provider's office? If so, is there difficulty?

- Does the patient utilize assistive devices?

- How far does the patient walk before dyspnea or desaturation occurs?

- Is the patient bedbound?

- Is there familial involvement?

- What is the patient's acuity level? How many comorbidities?

My Story: I often get calls from family members who say that their loved ones have PCPs but the loved one can't get out to see the PCP because of X. This is important; you want to document your note accordingly and send the note to the patient's PCP. This will demonstrate that you are not soliciting or trying to steal other providers' patients. Most of the one-time consult calls such as this come from my website.

I strongly suggest that you make sure that a Medicare patient who requires a house call gets a thorough phone triage before you actually make the visit. The phone triage can be a simple list of questions such as (1) Do you drive? (2) Do you utilize any assistive devices for ambulation? and (3) Are you on oxygen? I suggest a simple line of questioning before you visit the Medicare Part B beneficiary because if you can determine if the patient is truly homebound *before* you make a house call, this will not only save you a wasted visit but will prevent a negative outcome during an audit for medical necessity.

Chapter

16

Louisiana Lagniappe

❦

"There is no royal, flower-strewn path to success. And if there is, I have not found it. For if I have accomplished anything in life, it is because I have been willing to work hard."

—Madam C.J. Walker

It's already been 10 years of practice for me, and it's been a great run. I have learned much about myself as a person and as a clinician. I never started out to be a business owner. I honestly just wanted to help people and to make enough money to buy some sandwiches and pay the rent (this was before I was married). What happened to my practice with the growth, the ebbs and the flows, made me better as a whole. I have no regrets. I can honestly say from the most visceral part of me that I would do it all over again, because I started with a passion for the people and a love of nursing. The business side of things was something I fought, but that I had to learn if I wanted to remain alive and eating.

You won't get wealthy by making house calls, but your spirit will be filled. You won't have a skyline office view, but you will have the cutest 105-year-old lady dressed in her Sunday best with a pot of sweet peppermint tea waiting on you when you arrive for that house call because she knows it's your favorite. It doesn't get any better.

As I conclude, I want to leave you with some final thoughts, the most essential things to keep in mind at all times as a house-call practitioner.

- If you're going to be late, please have your staff call. Most of the patients will skip B-I-N-G-O to wait for you.

- If you can't make the visit, promptly reschedule.

- Don't solicit. This means don't get involved in fraudulent attempts to lure patients to your practice.

- Always keep your eyes peeled for dogs or other animals that may be on the prowl in the neighborhood. Dogs, wolves, and bees have personally chased me.

- If you don't feel safe, keep driving.

- Be mindful of fabric covered chairs, sofas, etc. These items can mask wet spots. It's best to stand if you can't readily determine if there is hidden moisture, especially if a floral pattern is involved.

- Don't forget to pack a few healthy treats if you will have a long ride and not many places to stop. I will often bring a small cooler filled with grapes, granola, and water.

- Don't assume that homebound patients won't go to specialists; let them decide.

- Don't be afraid to consider hospice for your patients. Hospice is a beautiful option for patients with terminal diagnoses when home health is no longer a viable alternative. I often refer patients to hospice and follow those patients once they are admitted to a hospice program.

- Pets are family too.

- Be accessible. It's okay to give your cell number.

- We sometimes perform errands, write letters explaining why the patient can't perform jury duty, write letters for disability, and more. We charge $10–$15 for each depending on the patient. Everything is weighed on a case-by-case basis.

- We make an effort to send out birthday cards to all patients.

- We make an effort to send out sympathy cards to family members when our patients have died. I also attend some funerals when possible.

- Every home has a culture. Respect each home. This means taking off your shoes when asked, or respecting Sabbath hours where applicable, for example.

- Have fun. Drink tea and really get to know your patients. This is the most endearing thing ever, to sip tea and talk about life, family, health care, and comorbidities with your patients.

Appendix

Billing Codes

❧

House-Call Codes

The following items are the specific codes utilized for Primary Care Medical Home visits only. Do *not* use Office Visit codes. Also remember that the Place of Service (POS) code for medical house calls is 12. These are E&M codes commonly used by NPs, PAs, MDs, podiatrists, and anyone else who is able to assess, diagnose, plan, treat, and prescribe medicines for a patient. If you are an RN or anyone else working in home health, these are not codes that you would use.

The coding information below is from CMS (2013a) and AMDA (2014).

New Patients

99341: Home visit for the evaluation and management of a new patient, which requires these three key components: a problem-focused history, a problem-focused examination, and straightforward medical decision making. Counseling and/or coordination of care with other physicians, other qualified healthcare professionals, or agencies is provided consistent with the nature of the problem(s) and the patient's and/or family's needs. Usually, the presenting problem(s) are of low severity. Typically, 20 minutes are spent face-to-face with the patient and/or family.

99342: Home visit for the evaluation and management of a new patient, which requires these three key components: an expanded problem-focused history, an expanded problem-focused examination, and medical decision making of low complexity. Counseling and/or coordination of care with other physicians, other qualified healthcare professionals, or agencies is provided consistent with the nature of the problem(s) and the patient's and/or family's needs. Usually, the presenting problem(s) are of moderate severity. Typically, 30 minutes are spent face-to-face with the patient and/or family.

99343: Home visit for the evaluation and management of a new patient, which requires these three key components: a detailed history, a detailed examination, and medical decision making of moderate complexity. Counseling and/or coordination of care with other physicians, other qualified healthcare professionals, or agencies is provided consistent with the nature of the problem(s) and the patient's and/or family's needs. Usually, the presenting problem(s) are of moderate to high severity. Typically, 45 minutes are spent face-to-face with the patient and/or family.

99344: Home visit for the evaluation and management of a new patient, which requires these three com- ponents: a comprehensive history, a comprehensive examination, and medical decision making of moderate complexity. Counseling and/or coordination of care with other physicians, other qualified healthcare professionals, or agencies is provided consistent with the nature of the problem(s) and the patient's and/or family's needs. Usually, the presenting problem(s) are of high severity. Typically, 60 minutes are spent face-to-face with the patient and/or family.

99345: Home visit for the evaluation and management of a new patient, which requires these three key components: a comprehensive history, a comprehensive examination, and medical decision making of high complexity. Counseling and/or coordination of care with other physicians, other qualified healthcare professionals, or agencies is provided consistent with the nature of the problem(s) and the patient's and/or family's needs. Usually, the patient is unstable or has developed a significant new problem requiring immediate physician attention. Typically, 75 minutes are spent face-to-face with the patient and/or family.

Established Patients

99347: Home visit for the evaluation and management of an established patient, which requires at least two of these three key components: A problem-focused interval history, a problem-focused examination, straightforward medical decision making. Counseling and/or coordination of care with other physicians, other qualified healthcare professionals, or agencies is provided consistent with the nature of the problem(s) and the patient's and/or family's needs. Usually, the presenting problem(s) are self-limited or minor. Typically, 15 minutes are spent face-to-face with the patient and/or family.

99348: Home visit for the evaluation and management of an established patient, which requires at least two of these three key components: an expanded problem-focused interval history, an expanded problem-focused examination, medical decision making of low complexity. Counseling and/or coordination of care with other physicians, other qualified healthcare professionals, or agencies is provided consistent with the nature of the problem(s) and the patient's and/or family's needs. Usually, the presenting problem(s) are of low to moderate severity. Typically, 25 minutes are spent face-to-face with the patient and/or family.

99349: Home visit for the evaluation and management of an established patient, which requires at least two of these three key components: a detailed interval history, a detailed examination, and medical decision making of moderate complexity. Counseling and/or coordination of care with other physicians, other qualified healthcare professionals, or agencies is provided consistent with the nature of the problem(s) and the patient's and/or family's needs. Usually, the presenting problem(s) are moderate to high in severity. Typically, 40 minutes are spent face-to-face with the patient and/ or family.

99350: Home visit for the evaluation and management of an established patient, which requires at least two of these three key components: a comprehensive interval history, a comprehensive examination, and medical decision making of moderate to high complexity. Counseling and/or coordination of care with other physicians, other qualified healthcare professionals, or agencies is provided consistent with the nature of the problem(s) and the patient's and/or family's needs. Usually, the presenting problem(s) are of moderate to high severity. The patient may be unstable or may have developed a significant new problem requiring immediate physician attention. Typically, 60 minutes are spent face- to-face with the patient and/or family.

Domiciliary Codes

Domiciliary care refers to a facility that provides room, board, and other personal-assistance services, generally on a long-term basis. These facilities, often referred to as adult-living facilities and assisted-living facilities, do *not* have a medical component. They have a RN or a LPN that is the administrator, but their job consists of case management, risk management, and quality assurance, just to name a few. These administrators do not administer medications or dress wounds. If any of these services are needed, the facility will contract it out to third-party vendors.

The following coding information was retrieved from the CMS (2013a) and from AMDA (2014).

New Patients

99324: Domiciliary or rest home visit for the evaluation and management of a new patient, which requires these three key components: a problem-focused history, a problem-focused examination, and straightforward medical decision-making. Counseling and/or coordination of care with other physicians, other qualified healthcare professionals, or agencies is provided consistent with the nature of the problem(s) and the patient's and/or family's needs. Usually, the presenting problem(s) are of low severity. Typically, 20 minutes are spent with the patient, family, and/or caregiver.

99325: Domiciliary or rest home visit for the evaluation and management of a new patient, which requires these three key components: an expanded problem-focused history, an expanded problem-focused examination, and medical decision making of low complexity. Counseling and/or coordination of care with other physicians, other qualified healthcare professionals, or agencies is provided consistent with the nature of the problem(s) and the patient's and/or family's needs. Usually, the presenting problem(s) are of moderate severity. Typically, 30 minutes are spent with the patient, family, and/or caregiver.

99326: Domiciliary or rest home visit for the evaluation and management of a new patient, which requires these three key components: a detailed history, a detailed examination, and medical decision making of moderate complexity. Counseling and/or coordination of care with other physicians, other qualified healthcare professionals, or agencies is provided consistent with the nature of the problem(s) and the patient's and/or family's needs. Usually, the presenting problem(s) are of moderate to high severity. Typically, 45 minutes are spent with the patient, family, and/or caregiver.

99327: Domiciliary or rest home visit for the evaluation and management of a new patient, which requires these three key components: a comprehensive history, a comprehensive examination, and medical decision making of moderate complexity. Counseling and/or coordination of care with other physicians, other qualified healthcare professionals, or agencies is provided consistent with the nature of the problem(s) and the patient's and/or family's needs. Usually, the presenting problem(s) are of high severity. Typically, 60 minutes are spent with the patient, family, and/or caregiver.

99328: Domiciliary or rest home visit for the evaluation and management of a new patient, which requires these three key components: a comprehensive history, a comprehensive examination, and medical decision making of high complexity. Counseling and/or coordination of care with other physicians, other qualified healthcare professionals, or agencies is provided consistent with the nature of the problem(s) and the patient's and/or family's needs. Usually, the patient is unstable or has developed a significant new problem requiring immediate physician attention. Typically, 75 minutes are spent with the patient, family, and/or caregiver.

Established Patients

99334: Domiciliary or rest home visit for the evaluation and management of a new patient, which requires at least two of these three key components: a problem-focused interval history, a problem-focused examination, straightforward medical decision making. Counseling and/or coordination of care with other physicians, other qualified healthcare professionals, or agencies is provided consistent with the nature of the problem(s) and the patient's and/or family's needs. Usually, the presenting problem(s) are self-limited or minor. Typically, 15 minutes are spent with the patient, family, and/or caregiver.

99335: Domiciliary or rest home visit for the evaluation and management of an established patient, which requires at least two of these three key components: an expanded problem-focused interval history, an expanded problem-focused examination, medical decision making of low complexity. Counseling and/or coordination of care with other physicians, other qualified healthcare professionals, or agencies is provided consistent with the nature of the problem(s) and the patient's and/or family's needs. Usually, the presenting problem(s) are of low to moderate complexity. Typically, 25 minutes are spent with the patient, family, and/or caregiver.

99336: Domiciliary or rest home visit for the evaluation and management of an established patient, which requires at least two of these three key components: a detailed interval history, a detailed examination, and medical decision making of moderate complexity. Counseling and/or coordination of care with other physicians, other qualified healthcare professionals, or agencies is provided consistent with the nature of the problem(s) and the patient's and/or family's needs. Usually, the presenting problem(s) are of moderate to high severity. Typically, 40 minutes are spent with the patient, family, and/or caregiver.

99337: Domiciliary or rest home visit for the evaluation and management of an established patient, which requires two of these three key components: a comprehensive interval history, a comprehensive examination, medical decision making of moderate to high complexity. Counseling and/or coordination of care with other physicians, other qualified healthcare professionals, or agencies is provided consistent with the nature of the problem(s) and the patient's and/or family's needs. Usually, the presenting problem(s) are of moderate to high severity. The patient may be unstable or may have developed a significant new problem requiring immediate physician attention. Typically, 60 minutes are spent with the patient, family, and/or caregiver.

Initial Preventive Physical Examination

The following information about the initial preventive physical examination and the annual wellness visit is from the article "Billing and Coding for the Medicare Annual Wellness Visits" (Ziehm, 2012).

G0402: Initial preventive physical examination, face to face with patient; this service is for new Medicare beneficiaries and must be performed within the first 12 months of Medicare enrollment. This is not a physical exam, even though the provider does measure and record basic vitals, but the patient *is* also eligible for an EKG screening (electrocardiograph: G0403-G0405) and aortic aneurism ultrasound (AAU) if he or she meets certain guidelines for these services. Often referred to as the "welcome to Medicare physical," this benefit is payable only once during an enrollee's lifetime. If a patient does not take advantage of the welcome to Medicare visit within his or her first year of Medicare enrollment, the patient loses the welcome visit benefit, and it can never be recovered.

Annual Wellness Visit

G0438: Annual wellness visit; includes a Personalized Prevention Plan of Service (PPPS), initial visit. Once a patient has had the welcome to Medicare visit, 11 full months must pass before the patient is eligible for the initial annual wellness visit (AWV). This visit can be performed any time in the patient's life but can be performed only *once*. If a patient did not have the welcome to Medicare visit within that first year of Medicare enrollment, he or she is still eligible for the initial AWV at any point in his or her life.

At the initial AWV, the healthcare provider will perform all of the key components of the visit and will record and discuss findings with the patient. Together, the provider and patient will devise a wellness plan and screening schedule intended to aid in maintaining or improving the health of the patient. The key elements include:

1. Establishment of the patient's medical/family history;

2. Measurement of the patient's height, weight, BMI (body mass index), blood pressure, and other routine measurements as deemed appropriate, based on the patient's medical and family history;

3. Listing of current providers and suppliers (for diabetic supplies, for example) that are regularly providing care;

4. Detection of any cognitive impairments the patient may have;

5. Review of a patient's potential risk factors for depression;

6. Review of the patient's functional ability and level of safety, based on direct observation of the patient;

7. Establishment of written screening schedule for the patient, such as a checklist for the next 5–10 years;

8. Establishment of a list of risk factors and conditions against which primary, secondary, or tertiary interventions are recommended or underway for the patient, including any mental health conditions or any such risk factors or conditions that have been identified through an initial preventive physical exam (IPPE), and a list of treatment options and their associated risks and benefits; and

9. Provision of personalized health advice to the patient and a referral, as appropriate, to health education or preventive counseling services or programs aimed at reducing identified risk factors and improving self-management or community based lifestyle interventions to reduce health risks and promote self-management and wellness.

My Story: Our EMR has all of these nine elements

from the AWV as a template. If your EMR does not have this, it can easily be created from the requirements listed above.

G0439: The AWV includes a Personalized Prevention Plan of Service (PPPS), subsequent visit. After 11 full months have passed since the patient's initial AWV (G0438), the patient becomes eligible for the subsequent wellness visit(s). The patient can request this visit every year, but *only after a full 11 months have passed*. If you try to bill before the 11 months have passed, your claim will be denied. The key elements performed during the subsequent AWVs include:

1. Updating of the patient's medical/family history;

2. Measurement of the patient's height, weight, BMI, blood pressure, and other routine measurements as deemed appropriate, based on patient's medical and family history;

3. Updating of the list of the patient's current medical providers and suppliers that are regularly involved in providing medical care to the patient, as was developed in the first AWV, pro- viding PPPS;

4. Detection of any cognitive impairments the patient may have;

5. Updating of the patient's written screening schedule as developed at the first AWV, providing PPPS;

6. Updating of the list of risk factors and conditions of which primary, secondary, or tertiary interventions are recommended or underway for the patient, as was developed at the first AWV, providing PPPS; and

7. Furnishing of appropriate personalized health advice to the patient and a referral, as appropriate, to health education or preventive counseling services or programs.

Additional Home Health Codes

The following codes are what the physician uses to bill the insurance companies for signing the 485. The billing of these codes is something you can do for your physician as a courtesy or give them to the physician for their own biller to process.

G0179: The recertification code, G0179, may be submitted when the physician signs the certification (i.e., recertifies the patient's need for home health care) after a patient has received services for at least 60 days (or one certification period). Code G0179 should be reported only once every 60 days, except in the rare situation when a patient starts a new episode before

60 days elapses and requires a new plan of care. The Medicare allowed amount for this service (unadjusted geographically) is $61.21. (Moore, 2001, p. 16)

G0180: The certification code, G0180, is reimbursable only if the patient has not received Medicare- covered home health services for at least 60 days. (This would be a new patient.) The Medicare allowed amount for this service (unadjusted geographically) is $73.07. The service includes the following:

- Review of initial or subsequent reports of patient status,

- Review of the patient's responses to the Oasis assessment instrument,

- Contact with the home health agency to ascertain the initial implementation plan of care, documentation in the patient's record. (Moore, 2001, p. 16)

Appendix

Successful NP/PA House Call Businesses

❧

I wanted to include information about successful NP/PA-owned house-call practices because when I started, I could locate only one or maybe two. Finding these practices was the hardest thing ever. The following practices are only a handful, but it will give you an idea of what some successful practices look like. Go to their websites and look around. Here are some snippets from their pages.

Advanced Medical House Calls, PLC

(www.advancedmedicalhousecalls.com)

Owners: Laura Wilkerson, APRN, and Dr. Mark Wilkerson, MD DO

Location: Michigan

Advanced Medical House Calls realizes that there is no place like home and that is why they provide comprehensive home-based medical care that minimizes the need for hospitalizations, re-hospitalizations or admissions to long-term care facilities, such as nursing homes and skilled rehabs. They provide home-bound clients with convenient, high quality medical care in the comfort, privacy and safety of their own homes. Their providers will provide you with a wide spectrum of the highest quality personnel and medical care available.

Affordable Medical Consultants

(www.affordablehousecalls.com)

Owner: Niesha Richardson, APRN Location:

Indiana

Affordable Medical Consultants, LLC, is based on the belief that our customers' needs are of the utmost importance. Our entire team is committed to meeting those needs. As a result, a high percentage of our business is from repeat customers and referrals.

Affordable Medical Consultants understand that visiting patients where they live is not only good medicine; it is also good for the soul! It is their objective to provide high-quality, continuous, comprehensive care to patients at home, whether it is the family house, nursing home, assisted living center, senior living apartments, or hospice house.

Affordable Medical Consultants' mission is to provide excellent medical health care and personal attention in a comfortable setting—your home!

Berkshire Mobile Practice

(www.berkshiremobilemedicine.com)

Owners: Jeff Kellogg, PA, and Dr. Charles D'Agostino, MD

Location: Massachusetts

The guiding vision was of creating a medical practice that would serve the elderly and/or frail patients in the com- fort of their own homes. They understand that for many, getting to a primary care doctor's appointment can create both financial and physical hardship. By seeing the patients in their homes, they hope to minimize these factors.

Health at Home Consultants

(www.healthathomeconsultants.com)

Owners: Cynthe Dumler, APRN, and Jamie Peters, APRN

Location: Nebraska

Health at Home Consultants is the first Nurse Practitioner owned house call practice in the state of Nebraska. They specialize in bringing high-quality, cost-effective healthcare to the Geriatric population in their home environment. Their Nurse Practitioners offer a valuable service to homebound individuals, resulting in a perfect niche to homecare.

The goal of Health at Home Consultants (HAH) is to provide home care medicine in one of the most rapidly expanding areas of healthcare. They give compassionate and coordinated care with the entire healthcare team; considerate attention to prevent unnecessary hospitalizations by providing regularly scheduled visits, and availability for last minute needs in the home setting. Health at Home Consultants can play a major role in the expanded healthcare delivery, by setting our sights on what is best for the future of our patients.

Manhattan House Calls

(www.medhousecalls.com) Owner: Denis Tarrant, APRN Location: New York

Denis Tarrant is a Board Certified Nurse Practitioner in Adult Health. Founded in 2004, Manhattan House Calls has performed over 20,000 medical home visits, and continues to provide high-quality, cost-effective care to homebound patients. Denis serves on the Board of Directors for The Nurse Practitioner Association of New York State. He is also a clinical instructor for many major Universities and Col- leges. Manhattan House Calls was recently named amongst the Top Nurse Practitioner Practices in the country by onlinenursepractitionerprograms.com. He is well known within his community for high quality, comprehensive care.

Appendix

Further Resources

❧

American Academy of Home Care Medicine

(Information from www.aahcm.org)

Since 1988, the American Academy of Home Care Medicine has served the needs of thousands of physicians and related professionals and agencies interested in improving care of patients in the home.

Academy Board member volunteers and members work to reduce barriers and enhance practice education. Notable successes include: fostering increased reimbursement, sponsoring multiple educational and scientific seminars, and providing the practice community with a variety of helpful publications.

Academy members include home care physicians—physicians who make house calls, care for homebound patients, act as home health agency medical directors, or who refer patients to home care agencies. Specialties include internal medicine, family practice, pediatrics, geriatrics, psychiatry, emergency medicine, and more.

Other members are agency directors of forward-looking large and small home care organizations, medical directors of managed care plans, nurse-practitioners who make house calls, physician assistants, and administrators of medical groups interested in home care.

Members come from all across the United States. We also have some international members. The Academy welcomes student affiliates and corporate sponsor-members from a variety of fields of interest.

Are you a nurse practitioner who has ever wondered how to start a house-call practice? Have you ever wondered how to get paid for making house calls? Have you ever just wanted to know how to incorporate HIT (health information technology) into a house-call practice? If you answered "Yes" to any of these questions, then The Housecall Course at Advanced Clinical Consultants, by Dr. Scharmaine Lawson, NP, is the program for you. The Housecall Course was designed to equip nurse practitioners and other healthcare practitioners with essential skills necessary for starting a house-call practice. The nurse practitioner will obtain critical knowledge on how to incorporate house calls into an already existing medical practice, or how to start an independent house-call practice.

The goal of The Housecall Course is to equip the practitioner with all necessary tools to establish a successful house-call practice through a *live* house-call experience coupled with didactic education. 16 CEUs are available from the AANP for nurse practitioners. For additional information regarding dates and cost, go to www.DrLawsonNP.com and click the The Housecall Course tab.

References

⤬

American Association of Nurse Practitioners. (2013). Improve Medicare patient access to home health services. Retrieved from http://www.aanp.org/images/documents/federal-legislation/issuebriefs/issue%20 brief%20-%20improve%20medicare%20 patient% 20access.pdf

American Medical Directors Association. (2014). Draft letter to WPS Medicare. Retrieved from www. amda.com/publications/ StateChapter.pdf

Blocker, J. (2010). A history of digital radiography. Retrieved from http://ezinearticles.com/?A-History-of-Digital-Radiography&id=4600271

Centers for Medicare & Medicaid Services. (2012). The national provider identifier (NPI): What you need to know. Retrieved from http://www.cms.gov/Out reach-and-Education/Medicare-Learning-Network-MLN/MLNProducts/Downloads/ NPIBooklet.pdf

Centers for Medicare & Medicaid Services. (2013a). Services incident to a physician's service to homebound patients under general physician supervision. Retrieved from https://www. cms.gov/Regulations-and-Guidance/Guidance/Manuals/ downloads/ bp102c15.pdf

Centers for Medicare & Medicaid Services. (2013b). Homebound status. Retrieved from http://www. cms.gov/Regulations-and-

Guidance/Guidance/ Manuals/downloads/bp102c07.pdf

Centers for Medicare & Medicaid Services. (2014). Non- Physician Practitioner (NPP) Payment for Care Plan

Oversight. Retrieved from http://www.cms.gov/ Regulations-and-Guidance/Guidance/Transmittals/ downloads/R999CP.pdf

Conant, R. (2013). Home health legislation reintroduced in U.S. House, ensures better patient access to care, removes barriers for nurses as qualified providers. Retrieved from http://www.capitolupdate.org/index.php/2011/06/home-health-legislation-reintroduced-in-u-s-house-ensures-better-patient-access-to-care-removes-barriers-for-nurses-as-qualifed-providers

Elmblad, S. (2014). EOB: Explanation of Benefits. Retrieved from http://financialsoft.about.com/od/glossaryindexe/g/EOB_def.html

Emanuel, E. (2013). The house call is "making a come-back". Retrieved from http://www.advisory.com/daily-briefing/2013/09/10/the-house-call-is-making -a-comeback

Entrepreneur. (2014a). An introduction to business plans. Retrieved from http://www.entrepreneur.com/article/ 38290

Entrepreneur. (2014b). Subchapter S corporation. Retrieved from http://www.entrepreneur.com/ encyclopedia/subchapter-s-corporation

MedicineNet. (2014a). HIPPA definition. Retrieved from http://www.medterms.com/script/main/art.asp?articlekey=31785.

Moore, K. J. (2001). An update on certifying home health care. *Family Practice Management, 8*(5), 16.

Reimbursement Task Force "Resident to" Work Group. (2012). Understanding Medicare Part B incident to billing: A fact sheet. *Journal of Wound, Ostomy and Continence Nursing,* *39*(2S), S17–S20. Retrieved from http://journals.lww. com/jwocnonline/Fulltext/2012/03001/Understanding_ Medicare_Part_B_Incident_To_Billing_.5.aspx

Rouse, Margaret. (2011). DICOM (digital imaging and communications in medicine). Retrieved from Healthcare IT Glossary: http://whatis.techtarget.com/ definition/DICOM-Digital-Imaging-and-Communi- cations-in-Medicine

Shulman, R. (2007). New Yorkers feel right at home with house calls. Retrieved from http://www.washington post.com/wp-dyn/content/article/2007/03/13/ AR2007031301485.html

Unwin, B. K., Andrews, C. M., Andrews, P. M., & Hanson,

J. L. (2009). Therapeutic home adaptations for older adults with disabilities. *American Family Physician, 80*(9), 963–968.

Unwin, B. K., & Tatum, P. E. (2011). House calls. *American Family Physician, 83*(8), 925–931.

Web Finance. (2014). Team, definition. Retrieved from Business Dictionary: http://www.businessdictionary. com/definition/ team.html

Webopedia. (2014). Search engine optimization. Retrieved from http://www.webopedia.com/TERM/S/ SEO.html

Yudkin, M. (2014). Business names really do matter. Retrieved from http://resources.saylor.org.s3.amazonaws.com/BUS/BUS203/ BUS203-5.2_Business-Names-Really-Do-Matter_files/ BUS203-5.2_Busi- ness-Names-Really-Do-Matter.html

Ziehm, A. (2012). Billing and coding for the medical annual wellness visits. Retrieved from http://www. mbrbilling.com/ blog/bid/133349/Billing-and-Coding-For-the-Medicare-Annual-Wellness-Visits

Websites

❧

1. American Association of Nurse Practitioners: www.aanp.org
    The most comprehensive website for nurse practitioners that includes resources on CEUs, legislation, and conferences.

2. Medical Economics: www.medicaleconomics.com A solid and trusted source for any clinician in business.

3. Physicians Practice: www.physicianspractice.com A great business source for any clinician.

4. Family Practice Medicine: www.familypractice medicine.com. A great site for solid business tips for the clinician. They now accept non-physician providers into the organization.

5. Prescribers Letter: www.prescribersletter.com
    This is a quick way to receive CEUs when you're on the go.

6. SFax: www.sfaxme.com
    This has helped with our transition into a nearly paperless office.

7. Dropbox: www.dropbox.com
    I love this site. You can store all documents across multiple devices, a must when you're on the move.

Other books
by Dr. Scharmaine Lawson

❧

Nola The Nurse® She's On The Go Series Vol 1 (available in Spanish and French)

Nola The Nurse® & Friends Explore The Holi Fest She's On The Go Series Vol 2

Nola The Nurse® Activity Book for Preschool Vol 1

Nola The Nurse® Activity Book for Kindergarten Vol 2

Nola The Nurse® Math Worksheets for Kindergarten Vol 3

Nola The Nurse® English/Sight Worksheets for Kindergarten Vol 4

Nola The Nurse® Math/English Worksheets for Preschoolers Vol 5

Nola The Nurse® Math Worksheets for First Graders Vol 6

Nola The Nurse® STEM Activity Book for 5-8 year olds Vol 7

Nola The Nurse® & Friends Explore The Holi Fest She's On The Go Series Vol 2 Coloring Book

Nola The Nurse® Remembers Hurricane Katrina Special Edition

Nola The Nurse® Remembers Hurricane Katrina Special Edition Coloring Book

Black Dot

Non-Fiction:

Housecalls 101: The only book you will ever need to begin your medical practice, Part 1

Housecalls 101: House Calls 101: Part 2 The Complete Clinician's Guide To In-Home Health Care, Telemedicine Services, and Long-Distance Treatment For a Post-Pandemic World

Housecalls 101 Policy & Procedure Manual

Culture Stories: Racism, Bias, and Prejudice in Nursing (soon to be released)